Lily's Way

Scrutable Chinese Cooking

by
Lily Lee Levin

with
Kevin Sinclair

Photographs by
Benno Gross

Acknowledgements

I would like to thank everyone who inspired and helped me to produce this book. On the inspiration side there stand, first and foremost, my husband and children whose love of Chinese food and whose high critical standards have kept me on my culinary toes for many years. I have also derived immense encouragement from the hosts of friends and guests who have graced our dining table over the years. Their gracious compliments and, more importantly, their eager assaults on my offerings led me to think that I could perhaps play a role in satisfying the West's hunger for access to one of the world's great cuisines.

On the help side, I would first like to thank the Management of the World Trade Centre Club of Hong Kong and its staff — particularly Miss Kitty Lee — who brought their famed energy and business acumen to this project. I am most grateful to them. Kevin Sinclair's interest, wit and understanding were indispensable to my undertaking and completing this effort. I would also like to thank Benno Gross for his artistic and creative photographic renditions of some of my kitchen productions. And Peter Cook and David Perkins of PPA Design Limited have my thanks for their kind and professional assistance on editorial and production matters. American Soybean Association graciously provided me with the photos of the soya bean plants.

Finally, my thanks goes out to Tex McCrary — a life-long friend whose unwavering faith in me has helped me in this and many other endeavors.

Contents

Foreword   7

Introduction   9

Method cooking   12

The happy cookers   13

Buying choi   15

Chinese cooking: What is it?   16

The importance of heat   17

Four glamorous dishes   20

What sort of Chinese?   21

A Chinese meal from a Western kitchen   21

Varieties on a simple theme   24

Culinary matchmaker   25

East meets West   27

Helping yourself   29

Trading culinary cultures   31

The possibilities of POSS   32

Then there is POSSSS   33

The evils of MSG   35

Pardon me!   36

Sweet and sours   37

Symbol of abundance   40

Stir frying — a vital art   41

What goes with what   45

The basic steps in stir frying   48

Staying out of the kitchen   52

Stripping the mystery   56

Knifemanship   60

Cutting methods   61

Steaming   63

Stretching what you've got   69

Egg Foo into a new dish   70

A living cuisine   73

Cold dishes   73

Dishes with picturesque names   80

The miraculous bean   82

The Yin and the Yang   88

Can you use a microwave?   88

Noodles   89

Stewing   91

Insulting yourself   96

Rice   96

Peking duck   99

The magic pancake   101

Everyone loves onion cake   104

The last word   104

Bridal soup   107

Mongolian BBQ   108

Mongolian fire pot   110

The cup that cheers   112

Desserts   113

Recipe Index

Chicken Specialities
Lemon Based Sweet and Sour Sauce for Chicken   28
Soy Sauce Chicken   28

Sweet and Sour
Tomato Based Sweet and Sour Sauce with Fish and Shrimp   37
Soy Sauce Based Sweet and Sour Sauce with Pork   37

Stir Fried Fish and Shrimp
A One-for-all Recipe for Stir Fried Fish or Shrimp Dishes   43
Yin Yang Shrimp   44
Fish with Wine Sauce   46

Stir Fried Meats
A One-for-all Recipe for Stir Fried Beef, Pork, Chicken and Lamb Dishes   49
Stir Fried Lamb with Scallions   54
Minced Beef with Green Peas   56
'Return to the Pot' or Double Cooked Pork   59
Mu Shu Pork   60

Spare Ribs and Egg-plant
Spare Ribs with Soy Sauce, Garlic and Honey   57
Egg-plants Peking Style   59

Steamed Dishes
Steamed Fish   64
Drunken Chicken   64
Steamed Egg-plants   65
Plain Steamed Chicken   68
Steamed Bean Curd with Minced Pork, Minced Chicken or
   Minced Turkey   68
Steamed Egg Custard with Shrimp   68

Egg
The Master Recipe for Egg Foo Anything   72

Cold Dishes
Sweet and Sour Cabbage with Dry Red Pepper   73
Sichuan Cucumber   76
Bean Curd   76
Bon Bon Chicken   77
Five Flavored Beef   77
Pork with Garlic Sauce   78

Dishes with Picturesque Names
The Lion's Head   80
Ants on the Tree   81

Pock-faced Old Lady's Bean Curd   81

Bean Curd
How to Make Soy Milk   84
Stuffed Fried Bean Curd Puffs   84
Pressed Dry Bean Curd with Beef   85
Bean Curd Family Style   85

Noodles
Chia Chiang Mein   89

Stews
Stewed Duck   92
Stewed Chicken with Chestnut   93
Stewed Chicken with Golden Needle   93
Stewed Beef with White Turnip   93
Stewed Lamb with Shallots   93
Soy Sauce Fish — Red Cooked Fish   65

Rice
How to Cook Rice   96
How to Cook Fried Rice   97

Northern Chinese Specialities
Peking Duck   99
The Magic Pancake   101
Onion Cake   104

Soups
Corn and Crabmeat Soup   105
Bean Curd and Spinach Soup   105
Sour and Hot Soup   105

The Way of the Mongols
Mongolian BBQ   108
Mongolian Fire Pot   110

Desserts
Eight Precious Treasures Rice Pudding   113
Almond Curd or Almond Jelly   114

Foreword

By Kevin Sinclair

Watching Lily Levin explain Chinese home cooking is akin to looking at a dynamo in action. It is also like attending a course in Chinese culture because as Peking-born Mrs Levin chops eggplants and shreds pieces of pork, her discourses range over a field of subjects almost as wide as China itself. And why not? Because food is the basis of Chinese society and the dinner table is the focal point of daily life.

The vivacious, sparkling Lily Levin is a walking encyclopedia of Chinese food. This is partly an accident of fate. Chinese cuisine, broadly, is divided into four regions. She has lived in all of them. As a girl, she grew up in Peking, the focal point of northern cooking. Her teenage years were spent in Chungking when that Sichuan city was the wartime capital of Free China. Working as a broadcaster in Taipei, she enjoyed the rich food of Shanghai prepared by the many chefs from the port city who had moved to Taiwan in 1949. And finally, in Hong Kong, she delighted in the delicate dishes and magnificent seafood of Cantonese cooking, the cuisine which most of the world thinks of as 'Chinese' food.

Cantonese food is, of course, Chinese. But that's like saying that Italian food is European cuisine and ignoring every other sort of cooking on the continent. What many people in the West forget is that China is more than a country; it is a vast subcontinent with a rich stew of different races, climates, customs and eating habits. Throughout China, the favorite meat is pork. But in the northwest many of the population are Muslim and their religion forbids them to eat swine. Cantonese dislike lamb (many cannot physically stand its smell) but in enormous areas of the northern provinces it is the staple dish for Mongols. The south is hot and wet and fertile. The north is frigid in winter, dry and, without irrigation, barren.

Why would anyone eat the fin of a shark? Simply because there was nothing else to eat and that's what staved off starvation. That's how we got the delicious dish that has developed into shark's fin soup. That's how we got many Chinese dishes — through desperation.

You won't find recipes for shark's fin soup in this book. The raw material of that dish may be a trifle difficult to come by in Chicago, Birmingham, Hanover or Melbourne. What you will find is a description of ways in which housewives and amateur cooks can produce fine Chinese foods in their kitchens — the same kind of good home cooking that hundreds of millions of Chinese are enjoying every day.

The author of this book is a remarkable woman. I have known Lily and Burton Levin for many years, long before he became Consul-General of the United States in Hong Kong. As the wife of one of America's leading diplomats in Asia, Lily Levin is pressed into a frantic social round. When she has a free night she likes to stay home and cook something simple — perhaps a dish like bean curd with vegetable with some left-over chicken shredded on top.

But because she is the wife of America's top diplomat in Hong Kong, Lily Levin feels it is her duty to share her heritage of Chinese cooking with American women who have not long been in East Asia. She holds classes in her home and other venues in conjunction with the American Women's Association of Hong Kong. Attending them is a tremendous amount of fun. It's also extremely informative. Her knowledge combined with her personality make her an outstanding teacher. Listening to her lecture and watching her cook can be as enjoyable as eating the dishes she has prepared.

I have eaten and loved Chinese food for many years in places as different as luxurious restaurants in Taipei, grubby dockside stalls in Hong Kong, street markets in Malaysia and on fishing boats in the South China Sea. Banquets costing thousands of dollars a table are great affairs to mark weddings, anniversaries or Lunar New Year celebrations.

But when it comes to really satisfying food it is impossible to improve on sitting down round a table with your family and friends and eating wholesome, succulent dishes of home-cooked Chinese food. My son, aged eight, agrees. We live in the New Territories of Hong Kong and we make frequent visits to the market-place in a nearby village. He picks out his favorite foods and we take them home to cook them together. We're lucky, of course. We live in the world capital of Chinese cuisine. But the lesson that Lily Levin preaches in this book is that anyone, any-where, can cook satisfying, genuine Chinese food with what they have in their kitchens.

If there are any secrets concerning Chinese food, she has simple solutions to them. "I'm trying to strip away the mystery from Chinese cooking," she says. That is what she does in this book.

Introduction

The idea of writing this book has been cooking for more than a decade, but the temperature and the ingredients were never quite right. I married a Westerner who is in the Foreign Service — not the Foreign Legion as my mother-in-law once thought — and together we have lived in many countries. We have been busy for years, entertaining guests at home; and then there were the children — a boy and a girl — with their demands on my time and patience. As a couple in the diplomatic service, we find that food and entertaining play a larger part in our life than most other people's. Indeed, at early ages our children eagerly imitated their parents by inviting friends over for functions. I can still remember vividly my three-year-old daughter coming home from nursery and announcing: "Mother, I have invited some friends over for tea tomorrow afternoon." Her suggestion for the menu: "Just biscuits and tea and maybe some crumpets and jam." It was the mid 60's, we were living in Hong Kong and obviously my daughter had fallen under the influence of her rosy-cheeked English nursery mates. Indeed, at that time my daughter resisted the idea of being an American and insisted she was an 'England'. Another time my son, aged four, came home and asked me if he could have a cocktail party for his friends. I agreed, of course, and when the appointed day came I chilled some fruit punch and lemonade, strung cherries and marshmallows on tooth picks for Old Fashioneds and Martinis, and popped an enormous amount of pop corn.

Today this little boy and little girl are both entering college and claim to be independent young adults. Their absence, combined with the patience induced by advancing years, prompted me to take the road of a happy cooker. My cooking has brought many smiles and much satisfaction to friends and guests and, of course, my family. It's a good feeling to produce such smiles and satisfaction by being creative.

I was born in a military and rather old-fashioned Northern Chinese family. As far back as I can remember, our house was full of people — friends, relatives, my father's subordinates and occasional or frequent callers. I don't remember ever having dinner with just the immediate family. We always had to feed a troupe of guests. Even during some difficult years in Chungking during the war, the house was full. My father was a very generous man who loved friends and enjoyed good eating. Some of this has rubbed off on me. I am very much people-oriented, and what better way to get people together than over good food.

How did I learn cooking? By experiment and experience, the latter starting from my early years when I observed master chefs in action. When I was three or four, my mother suffered various ailments that left her rather weak. Every day in the early morning, after I was washed and dressed, I would be quietly led to the very last courtyard of the house to stay and play until dusk when I would be brought back to the front part of the house for dinner and then bed. In the back courtyard the servants had to figure out ways to keep me entertained so that I would not disturb my mother while she was resting.

In the early part of morning, I remember, I was given a few of my mother's pretty handkerchiefs to wash in company with the wash amah who would be doing the family laundry.

I would then get on to another chore — cooking — and would be given a small, dull knife and some vegetables to cut and play with. As soon as I got bored with this, I was moved on to another job — playing with dough. I had my little board and my rolling pin, and I was taught to make all kinds of dumplings and breads and all shapes of noodles (as Northern Chinese we ate wheat products every day). I would soon get tired of that game and insist on being carried piggy-back style. From this elevated position I would watch the family cook preparing lunch or making bread. When I became impatient with just watching, the cook would placate me with another contrived chore. He would give me a handful of ingredients and, on cue, I would drop them into the hot wok. Some people say that apprenticeship to a cook should begin at about eleven or twelve years of age. I started

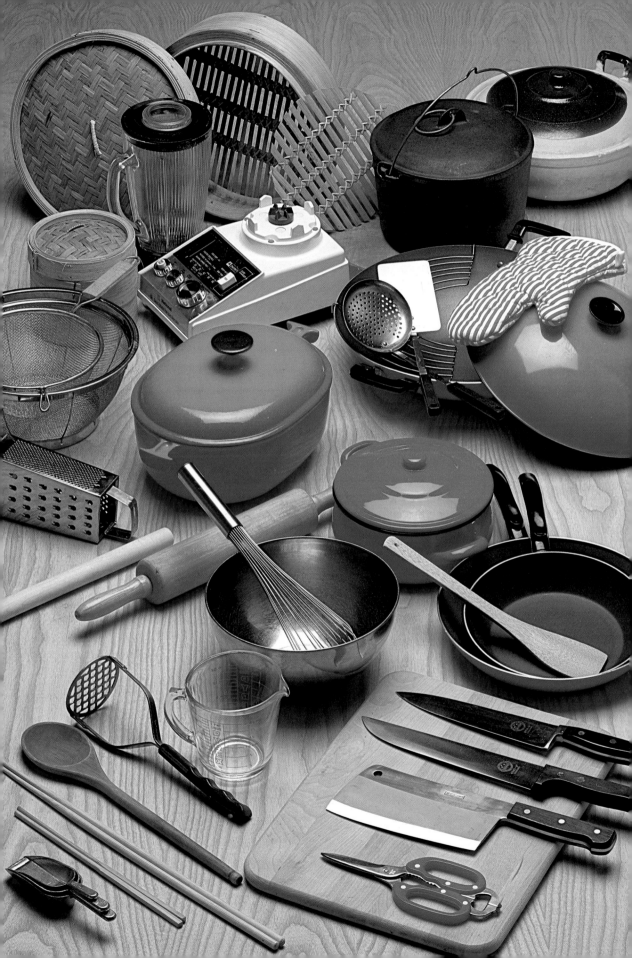

much younger. After I started nursery school, at the ripe age of five, I was considered too old a girl to hang around the male cooks. The kitchen became off limits for me, so there went my culinary education for the time being. After getting married in the States, I returned to the kitchen. It was like reliving my childhood, 'playing' with dough, cutting up vegetables and stirring away. The only not so much fun part was that I couldn't walk away from the mess and expect someone else to clean up. But after years of experience, I have developed short cuts which reduce the mess.

Today we live in the fast and processed food society. Our children grow up thinking fish are fillets and chickens come only in parts without heads and feet. To many in this day and age, meals are either something thrown together from frozen and canned ingredients or grabbed on a visit to a pizza or hamburger joint. Modern home makers strive to stay away from the kitchen or spend as little time there as possible. This is seen as an accomplishment, but the downfall of the role of the kitchen and the family dinner saddens me. Somehow I think of the kitchen as the activity and communication center for the family. Where did we leave messages for our children when we were not home to greet them? On the refrigerator door, of course. My kids always hung around the kitchen and brought their friends there in expectation of tasty treats. I recall that when we lived in Washington D.C., my son's fellow cub scouts crowded around the stove to watch me stir fry vegetables in what to them was a novel sight. I gave them all a taste of the finished product, and before long every one of their mothers had called to ask me how to make the vegetables which their sons had liked so much. Soon the families of the entire troop and many of their neighbors were talking about and making vegetables 'Lily's way'. This book seeks to spread the word on Lily's way a little further beyond the suburbs of Washington, D.C.

Method cooking

Since I am taking a method approach rather than a recipe approach to Chinese cooking, I would like to suggest that you read this book through before you rush into the kitchen. If you do, you will have a better understanding of my basic approach — which will make working with my recipes that much easier.

The happy cookers

When I have a group of people attending one of my study groups on Chinese home cooking, I call them 'The Happy Cookers'. This not only prompts a laugh but it also leaves people in a relaxed and happy mood. That is how people should be when they cook because cooking and eating are two of the great joys of life. Nobody should approach their kitchen in a bad mood. Cooking should be fun. It is like painting. An artist has to learn the basic techniques, how to use his brush to put oil on canvas. It's the same with Chinese cooking. Once you have mastered a few basics you can paint your own culinary picture. Everyone, even if not a culinary artist, is certainly a kitchen critic. And do not slavishly follow cook books. Not even this one. Express yourself. Use your imagination. Make a statement when you cook a dish. Show your individuality. Adapt recipes to what you want. If a recipe calls for pepper and you do not like pepper, don't use it. If you like things a little sweeter, use a bigger pinch of sugar. If your taste is for something with a bit of bite, use some red chillies. Remember, you are the cook and the recipe is there only as a guide, not as a commandment that must be followed to the letter. Remember the old Chinese saying that everyone's taste in food is different. Develop your own.

HOW TO BEGIN

Begin now for tonight's dinner. Try a few stir fried vegetables to go with your roast chicken or chops or whatever meat you are planning to serve. Look in your refrigerator. Cauliflower, string beans, carrots, cabbage, zucchinis — any one will do. Just follow the basic stir fry method on page 49. You'll find that with the same effort (or even less) that went into the old way of cooking vegetables, you can end up with a much tastier product.

Buying choi

All Chinese are vegetable lovers. And with the increasing international popularity of Chinese cuisine, it is becoming easier to buy genuine Oriental vegetables known as 'choi' and such examples as choi sum and bak choi are available in Chinatown markets. Don't put yourself through the inconvenience of a trip to Chinatown. Local vegetables can be used just as well and they will be considerably cheaper. So, stick to what you can buy in the local supermarket.

The Chinese culinary invasion of the world has meant that things like canned bamboo shoots are readily available almost everywhere. Use them. Don't bother to buy the expensive and hard-to- get fresh shoots. As a rule of thumb, frozen vegetables can be used in your Chinese family cooking. Generally, canned vegetables are out. But, as I have stressed elsewhere, it's all a matter of personal preference and common sense.

Another shopping tip: if you can't buy fresh hot red peppers, get a bottle of pepper flakes from your supermarket. The results will be the same.

Chinese cooking: What is it?

People often talk about 'Chinese' food. What is it? It can be many things to many people. The sheer vast size of the country ensures that there are going to be great varieties in the foods of different regions.

The south is sub-tropical and borders rich seas. So seafood is naturally going to take pride of place in the Cantonese kitchen. People enjoy fresh fish and vegetables and other ingredients all year round, so there is little need for spices or condiments to bring out the full flavor of the food.

The northern provinces are ice-bound for three months of the year and people exist largely on turnips and cabbages in the winter. So Peking chefs have devised many ways to make these basics tasty and edible.

The Shanghai area is a rich agricultural region and is known for its fine wines. The majority of Shanghai dishes include wine. Also, the Shanghainese have a sweet tooth and use a lot of sugar in their cooking.

Two thousand miles up the Yangtze river, the people of Sichuan make heavy use of hot red pepper. One reason for this is that the climate there is damp and the Chinese believe that hot red pepper is healthy for you in a damp climate. Another, and probably more basic, reason for the use of red pepper in such places as Sichuan, Kweichou and Hunan is poverty. The cheap red pepper stretches the food supply and adds life to what otherwise would be a monotonous diet.

These are examples from the four major regions into which Chinese cuisine is commonly divided, but there are many other local differences which can be found in the huge spread of China. Something to keep in mind is that people anywhere in the world can cook the good, honest home cooking of China because no matter where you may live there is some part of China that has a similar climate to you and probably produces the same sort of foodstuffs.

It is a common belief that all Chinese eat rice. Not true. Half the Chinese people in China seldom, if ever, eat rice. In my mother's kitchen, we ate rice as Westerners do; in puddings. In the north, flour from wheat, corn, soya bean or other sources is used to make pancakes, dumplings and bread. As in the United States, rice grows in the south and is largely a southern staple.

The importance of heat

If there *is* any secret to Chinese cooking it is the heat of the cooking flame. In the old days, this usually came from wood or charcoal. That explains the shape of the traditional wok, the curved Chinese pan used for stir frying, the basic technique for most dishes. The wok is round and has two ears to lift it because it was designed to fit into a hole on the top of an earthen stove, fitting as close as possible to the source of heat. The more intense the heat, the better. That's why it is no use trying to use a wok on an electric stove. There is too little point of contact between the rounded bottom and the hot plate. If you have an electric stove you are better off using a common Western frying pan. It gets more heat from the element and spreads it more swiftly and evenly. A wok is nice to use on a gas stove, but it is not essential. If you don't have one, don't worry. You don't need one. What you do need, though, is a reliable source of heat. In many cities, the heat and flames from your gas stove will change during the day. In mid-morning, the flame will be high. The heat will be intense. But at dinner time, when many stoves are in use, the flame will be lower. This makes a difference to what you are trying to cook.

The heat is the trickiest part of Chinese cooking. You can prepare ingredients in advance, but if you cannot cook them at the right temperature, your dish is not going to taste the way it should.

The rule is: the hotter the wok the better you can stir fry.

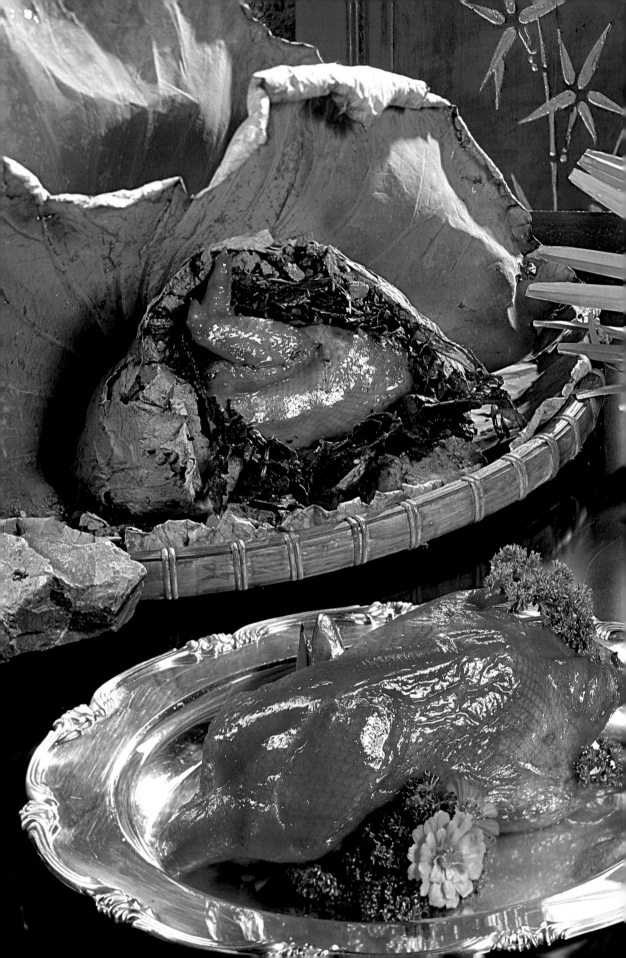

Four glamorous dishes

SUCKLING PIG

When Southern Chinese want to lay on a really impressive feast, the main dish of the meal is likely to be this imposing and delicious creation. The firm, crisp crackling is one course in itself and the juicy, tender meat accompanies a wealth of vegetable dishes. Truly, a dish fit for a prince — so much so that I have not attempted to give you a recipe for it in this book as you would be better advised to enjoy it in full when dining out.

PEKING DUCK

This most classic of all Northern Chinese dishes is also possibly one of the most famous — and with good cause, because it combines a beautiful appearance with a spectacular taste (see page 99).

BEGGAR'S CHICKEN

There are scores of legends about the origins of this colorful and unusual dish. One story has it that a poor man was sitting by a fire on the banks of a stream when a great lord came riding up with his entourage. The beggar was cooking a chicken that he had stolen from the other man's estate and he knew that his punishment, if he was caught, would be severe. So before the nobleman could get to him, he reached down into the stream for some mud and smeared the bird with a thick layer, then threw it into the fire where the mud baked into a rock-hard casing. The nobleman stopped to warm himself by the fire and chatted to the poor man. When he finally rode off, he tossed the beggar a handful of coins. The beggar — greatly relieved and by now very hungry indeed — retrieved the ball of mud, cracked it open and found his chicken, beautifully cooked, inside. The tender and succulent dish remains a firm favorite to this day.

SHANGHAI CRAB

In the brackish estuary of the Yangtze river live the creatures that constitute one of the gems of Chinese cuisine: small, dull-green hairy crabs — so called because of the fringes of fur on their legs and claws. Every autumn, train-loads of baskets full of the crabs head south towards Hong Kong where gourmets, eagerly awaiting their arrival, are prepared to pay as much as 10 U.S. dollars a crab to enjoy them, delicately steamed. Many Overseas Chinese are no less fanatic, often timing a visit to Hong Kong to make the most of both the crabs and the cool, autumn weather.

What sort of Chinese?

People often ask me what sort of food I cook. I tell them: 'Chinese.' "What sort of Chinese?" they enquire. "Family food from all over," I say. A typical family meal might be four courses and a soup served with rice or bread. It is Chinese custom to serve small portions of different meat dishes in one meal. What I like to do is produce a smorgasbord of Chinese cooking with a selection of dishes from the different parts of the country. I might do a cold Shanghainese salad as a starter, then a stir fried Cantonese vegetable and pork dish, a Sichuan diced chicken and red pepper, a Peking lamb stew and another dish from the south, a steamed fish. There's really no logic to this. Why should there be? But it's fun. It's good to eat. I enjoy it. So I do it.

A Chinese meal from a Western kitchen

In Washington a few years ago there had been a morning coffee gathering in a friend's home and, as lunchtime drew near, I said I would cook the gathering a Chinese meal. My friend protested loudly. "No, Lily," she said. "I don't have any Chinese food or cooking equipment. Let me go down to Chinatown tomorrow and we'll do it some other time."

Nonsense, I told her. *Every* normal American, European or Australian kitchen has the necessary equipment to cook a Chinese meal, and every Western refrigerator has the ingredients. I told her that I could go into virtually any Western house and cook a tasty, satisfying Chinese meal.

Let me give you an example. I went into my friend's kitchen and found the sort of layout and equipment that you could find in Kansas City or Capetown, Sydney or Santiago, London or Lisbon, Buenos Aires or Brussels. It was an average middle-class kitchen with a gas stove, a collection of pots and pans and saucepans, skillets and knives of various sizes and a cutting board. It is probably very much like your kitchen.

More important was what was *not* there. No wok. No steamer. No Chinese chopper. It was a typical Western kitchen. And the food I

found in the refrigerator was typical Western food. There were a piece of steak, two chicken breasts, some pork chops, two large green peppers and a dozen eggs. In the vegetable bin I came across some carrots, broccoli, a cucumber, garlic and onions. On the shelves above the stove there was a can of shrimps.

I was very pleased because here we had everything needed for the basis of a good Chinese meal. Soy sauce? No. Not necessary. Sesame oil? Likewise. There were salt, pepper, oil and sugar. And a bottle of vinegar.

That was all we needed. My friends watched in amazement as I made four dishes, food which is genuine Chinese family home cooking — sustaining, healthy, succulent and the sort of food that hundreds of millions of Chinese eat every day.

The four dishes were: egg foo yung (which simply means scrambled eggs with onions and shrimp or crabmeat); chicken with cucumber; pork with carrots and beef with broccoli.

The master recipe for egg foo yung is on page 72; and for the chicken, pork and beef recipes, you should follow the general stir fry instructions on page 49.

Total cooking time for the meal was 30 minutes. It looked impressive when it was served, but it was probably easier and more simple to cook than if the ingredients had been used to make a Western-style menu. I repeat: the secret of Chinese cooking is that it *is* simple. It's easy. Anyone can do it. And no matter where in the world you live, it is almost certain that you have in your kitchen at this moment the basis for a genuine Chinese meal just like someone is eating today in Peking or Shanghai.

LOOKING GOOD

First impressions count. How a dish looks is often as important as how it smells. So dress your dishes up a little. Decorate them. Make them look attractive. One way to do this which makes dishes look fresh and attractive is to scatter some sliced scallions on top. Other vegetables, like lettuce and sliced cabbage, can also be used to good advantage to make good food look good.

Varieties on a simple theme

You have probably got in *your* kitchen at this moment all the ingredients necessary to make 30 or more Chinese dishes. Let's take a look. We find a bit of steak, a couple of lamb chops and some chicken legs. You have carrots, garlic, beans, a green pepper and onions. There are some cans of prawn or crab.

What can you make out of these ingredients? An almost limitless selection of satisfying and tasty dishes.

With the steak as a basis, there are the choices of beef with onions, with green pepper, with green beans or with carrots. Or you could have beef with onion and green beans. Or beef with onions and green peppers. Or beef with carrots and green peppers. Or beef with carrots and green peppers and onions.

Turning to the chicken, you've got a similar range of choices. The same with the lamb. You can make a northern dish with a Mongolian flavor. Or you can combine the onion and beans to

make a vegetarian dish. Or beans and carrots. Some things, like beef and green peppers, go together naturally. But it is all up to the cook. It's what *you* want that matters.

KEEPING THINGS IN PROPORTION

Asians generally do not eat as much meat as Westerners. (Like every other generalisation there are exceptions to this statement; the Mongols are great meat eaters.) So when you are preparing a Chinese meal you should think about keeping things in proportion. About two parts of vegetable to one part of meat is a general rule of thumb to follow. Most Chinese eat many more vegetables than do Westerners. But I also have many Chinese friends who love the occasional juicy steak.

Culinary matchmaker

In old China, one of the most important people in the village or the neighborhood was the marital matchmaker. She knew everybody. She knew what skeletons were hidden in what family cupboards.

A good cook of family food should also be a matchmaker. He or she should know what will go perfectly with something else. There are no hard and fast rules; it depends on your personal taste. But there are a few general guidelines that are worth bearing in mind. Take garlic, for instance. In the family kitchen, garlic goes with green, leafy vegetables. But it does not go with more delicate white vegetables like cabbage or cauliflower. They call for the more refined flavor of ginger. Scallions go with almost everything.

Once again, it is just common sense. Do water chestnuts go with beef? Of course not. That's obvious to anyone. It is just as obvious that water chestnuts *do* go with shrimp or chicken.

But if you like garlic with your cauliflower, for instance, fine — have it. The only rule is to eat what you like. Rules are made to be broken. If you like something, break the rules.

Rice; Bean Noodles; Gingko Nuts; Soya Beans; Green Beans; Red Beans; Golden Needles; Bamboo Tips; Dried Shrimp; Chestnuts; Almonds; Agar Agar; Walnuts; Cashew Nuts; Dates; Wood Ear Mushrooms; Lotus Seeds & Lily Roots; Noodles

---

DEHYDRATED VEGETABLES

Many dried vegetables and other ingredients are used in Chinese cooking. In China, dehydration serves the same purpose as canning does in the West — it preserves and allows for convenient storage. When fresh vegetables are out of season or otherwise unobtainable, dried ones make good substitutes. Before using such dried foods as mushrooms, chestnuts, golden needles (a dried yellow flower in the lily family), wood ears (an ear-shaped fungus that grows on dead wood) and bean noodles (a transparent thin noodle made from the same green bean that produces bean sprouts), always soak them in hot water for about 15 minutes and then drain them dry for use. Chestnuts require special treatment. Soak them for about 3 to 4 hours, remove the brown skins, boil them for about 15 to 20 minutes, and they are ready for use.

East meets West

There are simple ways in which a bit of imagination can turn a leftover in your refrigerator into a Chinese delicacy. You may have some roast beef left over from the night before and friends have dropped in unexpectedly on a warm summer day. Here is an opportunity to give them an Oriental surprise.

Just cut the left-over roast beef into thin slices and arrange them on a plate. Sprinkle with a mixture of 2 to 3 tsp soy sauce, 1 to 2 tsp sesame oil and some chopped scallions.

On the other hand, Western food sometimes comes East. You will see in many cookbooks recipes for a dish called Lemon Chicken. It looks good. It tastes good. But it is not Chinese. It's like a European girl in a Ch'i P'ao (Chinese dress) — she may look terrific but she's not Chinese. There's nothing at all wrong with this sort of dish. People should experiment and cook what they like. With the basic skills you pick up from this book I hope you can give an Oriental twist to some of your favorite Western dishes or adapt Chinese dishes to your own taste.

Another example of chopsticks meeting the knife and fork is something which I quite often do at home: cook a Western-style roast and potatoes and then stir fry the vegetables Chinese style. My husband gets his meat and I get my vegetables and we are both happy. With a little experience, you will think of many combinations in which Chinese food and Western dishes can share the same table.

LEMON BASED SWEET AND SOUR SAUCE FOR CHICKEN

Use 1 lb of boneless chicken or 3 medium-sized chicken breasts. Cut the chicken into large bite-sized pieces, add salt and pepper to taste. Beat 1 egg with 1 tbsp each of flour and cornstarch. Coat the chicken with egg batter. Deep fry the chicken in 1 cup of oil for 3 to 5 minutes until it is golden brown and done, then scoop it out onto a plate.

To make the sauce: sauté 1 tsp of grated lemon peel (the yellow part only — the white part is bitter) in 1 tbsp of oil or butter. Add a mixture of 2 tbsp of sugar, the juice of 2 lemons, 6 tbps of water and 1 tsp of cornstarch to the saucepan, and mix and stir over medium heat for 10 seconds. Add the fried chicken pieces, mix well with the sauce, then remove from the heat and serve, topped with a few slices of lemon.

SOY SAUCE CHICKEN

You need one 2½ to 3 lb roasting chicken or fryer, or chicken parts, soy sauce, sugar, wine, ginger, sesame oil (optional) and water.

Clean the chicken or chicken parts and use paper toweling to blot the inside and outside dry.

Mix 3 cups of soy sauce, 3 cups of water, ¾ cup of sugar, ¼ cup of wine (optional) and a few slices of fresh ginger. Bring the mixture to the boil.

Immerse the chicken in the boiling sauce mixture (breast side down) and use a big spoon or ladle to baste it with the sauce.

Turn the heat to low (the sauce should be kept simmering and not allowed to boil rapidly), cover the pot with a lid, cook for about 25 minutes then turn the chicken over and cook for another 20 to 25 minutes with the pot covered.

Take the chicken from the pot, put it on to your cutting board and rub a little sesame oil over it. This gives a nice shine with a sesame flavor, but remember: don't overdose the chicken with sesame oil. If you don't have sesame oil, or don't like it, just use cooking oil to do the job.

To serve: chop the chicken, bones and all, into small pieces and pour some of the sauce from the cooking pot over it.

Hints
If you have any star anise and like the flavor, you can put a piece or two in the sauce mixture while the chicken is cooking. There is bound to be some sauce left over, so freeze it in a container and use it next time.

Helping yourself

Half the fun of a Chinese meal is eating it. "Naturally," you say. But the *way* in which you eat it is vital. *Never* serve Chinese food in individual portions and put these before your guests. That takes a lot of the fun and sense of companionship and friendship out of the Chinese way of eating.

Put your completed, cooked dishes on serving plates in the middle of the table and let people help themselves. If they don't like pork with red peppers, fine, they don't have to eat it. If they just adore chicken with cucumber and ginger and scallions, great, they can take more of that. Give your family or guests individual bowls of white rice, if you are serving it, and let them pick and choose what they want to go with it. Or, if you are concentrating on Peking food, put the pancakes or bread in the middle of the table and let them help themselves. As host or hostess, you may offer to help your guests to delicacies, pointing the way to those who may be unfamiliar with Chinese food.

But the fun is in helping yourself in a relaxed and informal atmosphere. If someone drops a chunk of beef and cauliflower on the table, so what. Table cloths can be washed. It's no big deal. The important thing is to enjoy what's in front of you.

And don't bother to spend a lot of money on a Chinese dinner set. You don't need it. You can serve your Chinese food on Western plates and bowls. Expensive table settings only show the wealth of the host. They do not improve the food, and in Chinese tradition it is the quality of the food itself that is of prime importance, first, last and always.

Trading culinary cultures

Just as the West has taken a lot from the traditions of Oriental cooking, so has China borrowed from other parts of the world. Take the tomato, for instance. It first made its appearance in China during World War II. The seeds were brought there by Americans helping China to fight the Japanese invaders. Nobody knew if the 'Foreign Red Persimmon' as it was called was a fruit or a vegetable. Some people ate it with sugar. Others stewed it with meat. But the tomato today is firmly established in the Chinese marketplace in the same way as the common potato, known as the 'Foreign Yam' (the Chinese only had yams) and other such vegetables as carrots and green peppers. In return, China has bequeathed the Western world such things as spaghetti, tea, ginger and bean sprouts. There is, however, one thing you will find in many Chinese restaurants in America that Chinese will never claim — the fortune cookie. That is purely an American innovation.

TRANSFORMING ITALIAN INTO CHINESE SALAD

Marco Polo got noodles from China so why shouldn't Chinese use Italian salad dressing as a basis for an exotic Eastern dressing?

Take your favorite Western salad dressing (not cheese or cream based) and add some soy sauce and sesame oil. Pour it over cold shredded chicken or pork with sliced cucumber and what have you got? An instant exotic Chinese salad.

THE BIG BASIC THREE

Garlic, scallions and ginger. They are the three basic items that will help you prepare magnificent dishes at home. Garlic is in most kitchens. You can always substitute ordinary onions for scallions, although the green leaves of the scallion help make your dishes look more beautiful and the taste is a little more delicate. As for ginger, if you can't buy fresh ginger where you live, supermarkets and delicatessens all over the world stock ginger powder. If you are really desperate, you can do what a friend of mine did in Denmark. She found it impossible to buy ginger in any form. So she went to a candy store and bought sugared ginger. She soaked it in cold water until the sugar had dissolved, then grated the ginger and used it to cook a Chinese home stew. She said it worked marvelously.

The possibilities of POSS

When you consider what basics you need to prepare genuine Chinese home cooking, think of POSS. It has limitless possibilities. Pepper. Oil. Sugar. Salt. These are the four vital items you need to prepare a Chinese meal. Are they in your kitchen? I'm sure they are, so you are already half way to cooking your first Chinese meal.

How much salt do you use in a dish of, for instance, chicken and walnuts and ginger? There is no hard and fast rule. It's exactly the same as when you are cooking a Western dish. Use your common sense. And taste the dish as it is cooking. A cook who does not taste the food while it is being prepared is not a good cook. It's the same with the sugar (almost *always* added at the last minute before the food is scooped out onto a serving plate). Sugar is not used as a sweetener, except for occasional dishes like sweet and sour, but as an item to enhance natural flavor.

Then there is POSSSS

After you have cooked your first few successful Chinese dishes you will probably feel a little more confident, a little more ambitious, and want to branch out a bit. Good. So in addition to POSS you might want to stretch your vocabulary by another S or two and add soy sauce and sesame oil to your kitchen cupboard. That's okay. No problem. I doubt very much if there is a supermarket in the United States today that does not stock soy sauce. Most would also have sesame oil. And they probably have a great deal more Oriental specialties that until a few years ago would never have been seen in an American store. The same goes for other Western lands because Chinese food is taking the world by storm. A friend told me recently that she thought there was a wok in every kitchen in California.

But a word of warning about sesame oil. It is a marvelous ingredient and adds the subtle hint of the Orient to the simplest of dishes. But it should be used sparingly. Too much sesame oil is like too much strong perfume on a hot day.

The evils of MSG

One very good reason for anyone to learn to cook Chinese family food is that it provides an easily-prepared, very healthy, balanced diet. And if you cook for yourself in your home, you have the added assurance that you know what you are eating. In too many Chinese restaurants all over the world, when you sit down to a meal, you are also going to be consuming large amounts of monosodium glutamate. This artificial material, known as MSG, is what is responsible for the so-called 'Chinese Restaurant Syndrome' which so many people complain of after they have eaten a Chinese meal.

If people are allergic to MSG — as many are without realising it — they may get terribly thirsty, their heart rate can get faster or slower, they drop off to sleep and develop blinding headaches.

Scientists are still examing this substance to see to what extent it is harmful. I don't care what their findings are; in my opinion, MSG will always be suspect. I never use it and if I go to a Chinese restaurant I always sneak out to the kitchen to check if it is going into the food. Often, what I see frightens me because chefs have been trained to use the substance and automatically put it into every dish. Why? It makes work easier for poor cooks using poor ingredients. Another example of this kind is the excessive use of baking soda in beef dishes.

In the old days, beef was a rarity on the Chinese table. It was just too expensive. And what little you did get tended to be water buffalo or old cow. Tenderiser was needed so baking soda was used to make the meat easier to eat.

Today, with excellent prime beef available everywhere, there is no need to treat beef with tenderiser. And yet so many cooks still use baking soda because that's what they were trained to do.

Pardon me!

Many years ago, a friend of mine from a Western country arrived to work in Singapore. It was the first time he had been in Asia and to welcome him to the East a group of his new workmates took him out for a meal in one of Singapore's truly magnificent outdoor restaurants where you dine under the tropical moon in the southernmost Chinese city on earth.

He had never before grasped chopsticks and as he wrestled with them (with a great lack of success) he noted the way in which the prawns and fish and other delicacies were rapidly disappearing. The other diners, both Chinese and foreigners who had lived for a long time in the Far East, were piling food in their rice bowls and scooping it into their mouths. What, he enquired, were the rules of Chinese table manners. An Old Asian Hand, an Australian who had spent most of his life in the East, finished his Singapore noodles and said: "Listen, mate, the first and last rule of Chinese manners is to make sure you've had enough to eat."

Not quite. But there's certainly more than a grain of truth in this lesson. Chinese table manners do not require the formalised elegance of dining in a three-star French restaurant. When you eat your rice, you *do* pick up the bowl to get the dish strategically closer to your mouth. Mothers will tell lazy children to lift their bowls instead of picking at their rice with the bowl on the table. You are less likely to spill the contents. But if the children should appear to be too greedy, the mother will sharply order them to put their rice bowls back on the table.

There are *some* formal Chinese table manners. But not many. Especially when you are eating with friends and family. The stress is as it should be, on enjoying yourself, on eating good food with good friends. And if your wayward chopsticks should drop a bit of juicy onion in the chilli sauce bowl, pluck it out and eat it. Who's going to complain?

The most important thing about good table manners is that nobody notices *how* you eat. Fancy, pretentious manners might make people feel as uncomfortable as sheer bad manners.

Sweet and sours

TOMATO BASED SWEET AND SOUR SAUCE WITH FISH AND SHRIMP

Use 1 lb of filleted fish, cut into bite-sized pieces, or 1 lb of cleaned and deveined shrimp. Salt and pepper to taste and mix well with 1 tbsp each of wine, cornstarch and flour. Deep fry the fish or shrimp in 1 cup of cooking oil for 2 to 3 minutes until it is golden brown, then scoop it onto a plate.

To make the sauce: sauté 1 tsp each of chopped garlic (about 1 clove) and ginger in 2 tbsp of oil in a frying pan or pot. Mix 1 tbsp of wine, 2 tbsp of sugar, 3 tbsp of vinegar, 4 tbsp of tomato catsup, 5 tbsp of water and 1 tsp of cornstarch and pour into the frying pan or pot. Stir for 15 to 20 seconds over medium heat.

Add the deep fried fish or shrimp to the sauce, mix and stir for 10 seconds, remove from the heat and serve.

SOY SAUCE BASED SWEET AND SOUR SAUCE WITH PORK

Use 1 lb of tenderloin or any lean pork cut into bite-sized strips. Salt and pepper lightly and mix well with 1 tbsp each of soy sauce, wine, cornstarch and flour. Deep fry the meat in 1 cup of oil for 3 to 5 minutes until it is brown and done, then scoop it onto a plate.

To make the sauce: sauté 1 tsp each of chopped garlic (about 1 clove), scallion and ginger in 2 tbsp of oil in a frying pan or pot. Mix 1 tbsp of wine, 2 tbsp of soy sauce, 3 tbsp of sugar, 4 tbsp of vinegar, 5 tbsp of water and 1 tsp of cornstarch and pour into the frying pan or pot. Stir for 15 to 20 seconds over medium heat.

Add the deep fried pork to the sauce, mix and stir for 10 seconds, remove from the heat and serve.

Hint
The art of arriving at a good sweet and sour sauce is, of course, to achieve the proper balance of sugar and vinegar or sugar and lemon. I have suggested to you the general method, but the

degree of sweetness and sourness is up to your particular taste. So when you prepare such a sauce for the first time, you should make your own adjustments and take a note of them.

Another hint
Since there is quite a lot sugar in the cooking, use medium heat and pay close attention to the sauce as it is cooking, because sugar is easily burned. Burned sugar will make your sweet sour turn into bitter sour. Besides, it gets stuck to the cooking pan, making it very hard to clean.

And another hint
If you like, you can also use ½ to 1 cup of various kind of vegetables, such as green pepper, peas, snow peas, onions, carrots, tomatoes, button mushrooms, or pineapple to mix in with your sweet and sour dishes. The best time to add these ingredients — sautéd together with ginger, scallion and garlic — is just before you pour the mixture of the sauce ingredients into the cooking pan.

Sweet & Sour Fish; Sweet & Sour Pork; Sweet & Sour Shrimp

Symbol of abundance

Fish is always served as the last course at a formal Chinese banquet. This is because the word fish is pronounced 'Yu' and the same sound is used for the word abundance. (The written characters, though, are very different.) So to demonstrate that it is a time of plenty, the symbol of abundance is eaten last.

In the north of China where I was born, the winters are very cold. The rivers freeze over so there are no fish. But the old beliefs were held so strongly that at the end of a fishless winter dinner a carved wooden fish would be carried to the table and covered with a rich sauce. This signified abundance — but the plump summer fishes tasted a lot better.

At the other extreme of China, along the fertile tropical coast bordering the rich fishing grounds of the South China Sea, there are other superstitions about fish. Around Hong Kong, there are people whose clans have not lived on land for generations. They are born on their junks or sampans, grow up on the water, marry on their boats and spend their lives afloat. These are the fisherfolk, people called Hoklo and Tanka. They never, never, never, turn over their steamed fish. Once it is on their plates they delicately pick out the meat with their chopsticks, lift the bone from the plate to get at the delicacies on the underside of the skeleton, but ensure that the fish is not turned over. They believe if it is turned over, their boats will capsize.

There must be thousands of stories about fish in Chinese family cooking. One fable illustrates how Chinese value fish. Steamed fish is best and the head of the fish is the sweetest. This delicacy was reserved for the old and the wealthy. Throughout her history China has been plagued by bandits, and the story has it that centuries ago a roving band of kidnappers decided to abduct the son of a wealthy landlord. They swooped on the village and made off with a boy. But had they got the right child?

Back at the bandits' hideout, their leader thought of a way to find out if the boy came from a rich or poor family. "Cook fish," he ordered. The gang sat down to eat with their victim. The boy reached out with his chopsticks and picked a portion from the head, the choice part of the fish.

"We will get our money," said the bandit chief.

Stir frying — a vital art

Nine out of 10 of the Chinese dishes you cook will be stir fried or an adaption of this basic technique. What do you need to cook a dish of Chinese food in this manner? A frying pan and a spatula. How do you do it? You put oil in the pan, heat it until it smokes and put in the garlic, salt or ginger to taste. Then you put in the ingredients, meat or vegetables, with those that need more cooking time going in first. Then you stir vigorously to prevent them sticking to the bottom of the pan. Does that sound difficult? Of course not. It's simple. And it's the single most important action in cooking most Chinese dishes. So much for Chinese cooking being mysterious and complicated.

My aim is to take the inscrutability out of cooking Chinese food. Of course, there is more to stir frying than I have outlined; you've got to know what goes into the wok or frying pan as the case may be. And, especially in some Shanghainese and Peking specialities, the stir fry method will become a little more sophisticated to allow you to simmer and stew dishes.

When you are cooking several stir fried dishes, you can often use the same pan without bothering to wash it. Naturally, if you have

cooked a dish with a strong flavor like beef and green peppers and plan to follow it with something delicate like chicken and cucumber, you are going to have to wash the pan before you start the second dish. But generally you can cook one dish, scoop it out on a serving plate and immediately start cooking another. Some people wash 10 pans to cook two dishes. This can become pretty tedious. It's also not much fun if you have to do the washing up.

A ONE-FOR-ALL RECIPE FOR STIR FRIED FISH OR SHRIMP DISHES

For fish or shrimp and vegetables, the proportion is 2 cups to 1 cup — i.e. twice as much fish or shrimp as vegetables.

Method
Clean the fish (which should be filleted and cut into bite sized pieces) or the shrimp (which should be deveined) and use paper toweling to blot dry.

Shrimp with Green Peas; Shrimp with Red Pepper & Scallions

Salt and pepper the fish (dusted with a little cornstarch as a binder to prevent it from falling apart while cooking) or the shrimp and separately dice, shred or slice the vegetables.

Proceed as you would with a meat dish — stir fry the vegetables for about 10 to 15 seconds in 1½ tbsp of heated oil, salt very lightly and then scoop the vegetables out of the pan. Add another 2½ tbsp of oil and when it is hot, sauté a few slices of ginger or, if you prefer, a little chopped scallion or garlic.

Add the fish or shrimp, stir fry for about 20 to 30 seconds until almost done, and put back the vegetables. Stir fry for another 5 to 10 seconds. Taste, add salt if necessary and a pinch of sugar, and it is ready to serve.

Hint
Ginger complements sea food. Use a lot of it when available. Sautéd ginger gives off a fragrant aroma and imparts a delicate flavor to the seafood. If you don't like ginger, substitute scallions.

Note
Fish and shrimp are often cooked with only a few slices of ginger and a couple of scallion stalks cut into about 1-inch lengths. With fish, soy sauce can be used instead of salt, but it is generally not used with shrimp since it would overwhelm the delicate flavor. If you use soy sauce, the general rule is 1 tsp for every cup of meat or fish.

HERE ARE A COUPLE OF STIR FRIED DISHES WITH SOME SPECIAL QUALITIES

YIN YANG SHRIMP

Stir fry the shrimp and scoop out half of it when cooked. Add 1 tbsp of catsup to the remaining half in the pan, stir for 2 seconds or so and scoop out. Arrange the shrimp in a dish, keeping the two portions separate. The colored shrimps are the 'Yin' or dark side and the uncolored shrimps are the 'Yang' or light side.

What goes with what

	Beef	Pork	Lamb	Chicken	Fish	Shrimp
Asparagus	x	x		x	x	x
Bamboo shoots		x		x	x	x
Bean curd (Tou Fu)	x	x		x	x	x
Bean sprouts		x		x	x	x
Broccoli	x	x		x		
Brussels sprouts	x	x	x	x		
Button mushrooms		x		x	x	x
Cabbage and Chinese cabbage	x	x		x		
Carrots	x	x	x	x		
Cauliflower		x		x		
Celery	x	x	x	x	x	x
Cucumber		x		x		x
Egg-plant	x	x				
Ginger (young)	x	x			x	x
Golden needle		x		x		
Leeks	x	x	x			
Mushrooms		x		x	x	
Mustard greens	x	x				
Nuts		x		x		
Onions	x	x	x	x		x
Peas		x		x		x
Pepper (green)	x	x	x	x		
Pepper (red)	x	x	x	x		x
Potatoes	x	x	x	x		
Scallions	x	x	x	x	x	x
Shallots	x	x	x	x		x
Snow peas		x		x	x	x
Spinach		x		x		
String beans	x	x		x		
Tomatoes	x	x	x	x	x	x
Turnip	x	x				
Water chestnut				x		x
Wood ear		x		x	x	
Zucchini		x		x		

Chicken with Walnut; Chicken with Dry Hot Pepper; Chicken with Shallots, Green Pepper & Black Soy Beans

FISH WITH WINE SAUCE

Follow the basic stir frying method for filleted fish. Just before you scoop out the fish, add ¾ cup to 1 cup of white wine (on the very sweet side or, if not, add sugar) into which 2 tsp of cornstarch has been mixed. Simmer for about 30 seconds to 1 minute. The dish should be very 'saucy' and rather sweet and full of wine flavor. Traditionally this dish is cooked with black wood ear, but you don't have to worry as the fish alone in the wine sauce is quite elegant and tasty. One other thing: during the simmering, you may wish to drop in a few green peas to add color.

Shrimp with Cucumber; Shrimp with Bean Sprouts; Shrimp with Bean Curd (Tou Fu)

1 Heat the wok or pan

2 Pour in the oil

3 Add the garlic/ginger/scallion . . .

4 . . . and quickly sauté to bring out the fragrance

5 Add the meat and stir fry

6 Remove the meat

7 Add the vegetables and quickly stir fry

8 Return the meat to the pan and stir fry for a few seconds

A ONE-FOR-ALL RECIPE FOR STIR FRIED BEEF, PORK, CHICKEN AND LAMB DISHES

Since the total concept of this cook book is a method approach rather than a conventional recipe approach, I do not want to bore you with recipes for every single dish. Besides there is no need to do that, for most stir fried dishes follow the same principle and use the same or similar spices. As you gain experience, you'll see that by adding or substracting one or two spices and putting different combinations of meats and vegetables together you can produce a large variety of dishes of different appearance, color, aroma and taste. For your convenience, I have included a chart of meats, seafood and vegetables which the Chinese believe go particularly well together, but don't feel completely bound by this. (The chart is on page 45.) Stir frying is one of the most important and yet most simple elements of Chinese cooking. Follow my suggestions and you'll be pleased to discover how easy it is to turn out a wide variety of Chinese dishes.

Here is my master recipe for all stir fried dishes containing meat. Do keep in mind my earlier description of Chinese cooking as the art of matchmaking. For meat dishes the standard proportion is

COOKING THE GREENS

When stir frying green vegetables, add a pinch of salt. This is not only for taste, it helps to retain the living green color when the dish is cooked.

twice as much vegetable as meat. Since meat is an expensive delicacy in overcrowded China, Chinese food traditionally goes heavier on the vegetables. But if you or your family are heavy meat eaters, tinker with the proportions even to the point of reversing them. No harm done — except to your food bills.

Slice, shred or dice 1 cup or about ½ lb of meat. Add a pinch or two of salt and pepper to taste (you can substitute 1 to 1½ tsp of soy sauce for the salt). Mix the meat and the seasoning together.

Slice, shred or dice 2 cups of various vegetables such as carrots, onions, snow peas, green peppers, cauliflower, broccoli and cucumber.

Heat 2 tbsp of oil in a frying pan, add the vegetables, salt them lightly and stir fry for 10 to 15 seconds. Scoop the vegetables out and leave the excess oil in the pan.

Add another 2 tbsp of oil, brown a few thin slices of ginger or a little scallion or garlic, according to your taste. Then add the meat, stir fry quickly in the hot oil and when the meat is almost done, add the vegetables and mix and stir fry for another 5 to 10 seconds. Taste to see if you need to add salt or soy sauce, add a pinch of sugar (yes sugar, to give a zest to the dish) and scoop the mixture out onto the serving plate.

Hint

Since everyone's taste is different, go easy at first on the salt or the soy sauce. You can always add more. Also always remember to taste the dish before it goes onto the serving plate as it's bad form to add salt or soy sauce after the dish is on the table.

TAKING A TASTE

When you are cooking, don't be afraid to pick out a piece of meat or vegetable and taste it to see if the ingredients have enough seasoning. How else are you going to tell if the dish is just right for you? If you wait until the food is on the table before you taste, it is too late to add that last gentle touch.

Remember that strictly speaking soy sauce is not a condiment to be put on the table. It is a seasoning to be used in cooking. When the dish is cooked properly there should be no need to put it in a bowl of soy sauce to get extra flavor. The taste should be cooked into the dish.

Staying out of the kitchen

You are expecting six guests for dinner and you want to be with them while still showing off your skill in Chinese family cooking? Good. Do what I do. Get as much of the work as possible done in advance. This will prevent any last-minute panic in the kitchen (or

SOME LIKE IT HOT

If you like to eat hot food, just add red pepper flakes or fresh red pepper while cooking to turn any dish into a Sichuan or Hunan concoction. How much red pepper to use is entirely up to you — depending on how hot you want to go. If someone in the family dislikes hot food, simply make a hot pepper sauce into which you can dip your food.

Here is a simple way for you to make a hot oil sauce — your own home-made Chinese Tabasco. Put 4 tbsp of red pepper flakes in a bowl, salt and pepper and add 1 tbsp of chopped scallion. Heat ½ cup of cooking oil and when it's smoking hot, pour it over the mixture in the bowl. Cool the mixture, put it in a small jar and store in the refrigerator. It will keep for weeks.

at least reduce it to a minimum) and allow you to spend the maximum amount of time away from it.

Let's visualise a typical menu.

How about a cold dish, prepared in advance and waiting in the refrigerator . . . a soup, also prepared in advance . . . a stew, pre-cooked and only requiring re-heating before serving . . . and a steamed dish in the process of cooking (or if you are using a steamer with two decks, you can steam two dishes simultaneously). So the cold dish is ready to go, the soup and the stew are on the stove, and the steamed dishes are steaming. All that's left for you to do is to make one or two stir fried dishes. With the ingredients already pre-cut and lined up, you'll need no more than a few minutes. Then, lo and behold, all the dishes arrive on the table

together and — almost before you can say 'Lily's Way' — you're relaxing, sitting down with your guests.

If you plan ahead and get things ready well in advance, you can prepare a feast like this with a minimum of fuss and trouble. And it will give both you and your friends the maximum of pleasure.

STIR FRIED LAMB WITH SCALLIONS

This is a very traditional Peking dish. It's a simple stir frying affair, so follow the basics. Mix soy sauce with shredded lamb — about 2 tsp soy sauce per ½ to ¾ lb of meat — stir fry in hot oil for 30 seconds. Add 6 or more stalks of scallion (shredded), quickly stir fry with the lamb, then scoop out and serve with pancakes.

The tricky part of all of this is to avoid overcooking the scallions. They need only a few seconds of cooking and if they are over-cooked, they will ruin the dish completely.

Stir Fried Lamb with Scallions

MINCED BEEF WITH GREEN PEAS

This is a little dish I invented for my children. It's nutritious and easy to chew, and it's also a sneaky way to get children to eat a lot of vegetables. My kids call it cat food because it's rather mushy, but they still love it. Indeed last year my son called long distance from his boarding school in the U.S. to Hong Kong to ask for the recipe. I expressed surprise over his willingness to spend so much money on a long distance call, just for a recipe. He said that months of institutional food had produced a craving for 'cat food' and he just couldn't wait any longer. Yet he could probably have bought himself a fine steak or lobster dinner for what the call cost him. Here's how to make it.

Stir fry ½ to ¾ lb of minced beef (or pork or chicken or turkey). When the meat is done, dump in 1 cup or more of peas, stir until the peas are warm, and salt and pepper to taste. Turn the fire off, pour 2 slightly beaten eggs into the minced meat and peas, and stir. The eggs will be somewhat cooked by the heat of the dish and will give the mixture a smooth and slippery texture, much to the enjoyment of most children.

Stripping the mystery

Westerners often say they would like to learn how to cook Chinese food but that it is too difficult. That is not true. The basic good home cooking of China is simple — far easier to cook than French food, for instance. But a veil of mystery has been drawn over the cooking of China. This has had the unfortunate effect of persuading too many people that it is too difficult for the amateur to produce Chinese dishes in their homes. But if you think about this for just a moment you can see immediately that it is an absurd notion because every day in China scores of millions of housewives are doing exactly that — cooking nourishing, healthy food for their families. And these women do not enjoy the sophisticated aids and modern equipment that is in most Western kitchens. So if they can do it — and they do — so can you.

I sometimes suspect the people who spread the idea that there is some sort of secret to Chinese cooking are the owners of Chinese restaurants or the authors of cookbooks. Certainly, many Chinese cookery books are needlessly elaborate and complicated. In many cases, if a recipe calls for 12 spices and herbs and condiments you need only the basic three or four. Recipes for straightforward dishes that a child could make, for example, cover pages of text in some cookbooks. If anyone reads these books and then decides that tackling a Chinese meal is too difficult, I can understand why. But the facts are that there is no mystery to Chinese food and if there are any secrets, they are ones to which there are simple answers. Any housewife with average competence in a Western kitchen can cook good, genuine Chinese food merely by using a bit of common sense and following a few easy rules. You have got everything you need in your kitchen right now.

If you live in a Western country, all the raw ingredients you need are on the shelves at the nearest supermarket. You do not have to make a visit to Chinatown unless you want to go to really exotic lengths. With the growing popularity of Chinese food in America, Australia and Europe in recent years, things like soy sauce and sesame oil — and many rarer commodities — have become commonplace items in corner shops.

SPARE RIBS WITH SOY SAUCE, GARLIC AND HONEY

Use 3 to 4 lbs of spare ribs. Salt and pepper lightly and rub all over with crushed garlic or garlic powder. Pour enough soy sauce over the ribs to coat them generously, and place them in a roasting pan. Then add about ¼ cup of water and soy sauce mixed together in equal parts, to keep the ribs from getting stuck to the pan. Roast in an oven pre-heated to 250 to 300 degrees for 30 minutes or more, depending on how large the ribs are. Turn the ribs to make sure that both sides are roasted brown. Dissolve 1 tbsp of honey in ¼ to ⅓ cup of hot water, pour over the ribs, baste, turn and roast for another 10 to 15 minutes. Use the same method to roast chicken parts or pork chops.

You can also use this recipe for outdoor barbecueing. Just marinate the garlic-rubbed spare ribs, chicken or pork chops in soy sauce for 20 minutes or more and grill as you would with any BBQ — but baste with honey water.

EGG-PLANTS PEKING STYLE

Slice 1 to 1½ lbs of egg-plant into large pieces and stir fry for about 1 minute. Salt and pepper very lightly, add 1 tbsp each of soy sauce, vinegar and water, 3 garlic cloves (crushed) and 2 stalks of scallions (coarsely chopped), cover and simmer until the egg-plant is very soft. Before serving, add sugar (somewhat more than a pinch) to cut the sourness down a bit, although the dish should taste slightly vinegary. If you want to turn this into a tasty meat dish, stir fry about ½ lb of sliced pork, add to the egg-plant and simmer together until done.

RETURN TO THE POT OR DOUBLE COOKED PORK

As the name implies, the pork is cooked twice. The result is one of the most popular spicy Sichuan dishes as far as Westerners are concerned.

Onion Cakes; Egg-Plants Peking Style; Spare Ribs with Soy Sauce, Garlic & Honey

Boil ½ lb of boneless pork with a stalk of scallion or a piece of onion, and a slice of ginger for 15 to 20 minutes, using just enough water to cover the meat. Take the meat out, let it cool and cut it into thin slices.

Slice 2 bell peppers (1 red and 1 green, if available), 2 hot chilli peppers, 2 stalks of scallion, 2 slices of ginger root, 3 crushed or sliced cloves of garlic and, if you have them, 3 or 4 leaves of head cabbage cut into large pieces.

Heat 3 tbsp of oil and stir fry the sliced pork for ½ minute. Then add the vegetables and spices, stir fry for about 1 minute and scoop the mixture out onto a plate.

Use the remaining oil in the pan (if not sufficient, add 1 tbsp of oil), add a mixture of 2 tbsp of Hoisin sauce (or 2 tbsp of soy bean paste with 2 tsp of sugar), 1 tbsp of hot chilli bean paste (or use chilli pepper flakes) and 1 to 2 tbsp of soy sauce, and stir fry for 10 seconds. Return the pork and vegetables to the pan, stir for a few seconds, taste and serve. This dish should be spicy and chilli hot.

MU SHU PORK

Following the basic stir fried meat recipe, stir fry ½ lb of shredded or sliced pork loin, add 1 cup each of pre-soaked wood ear and golden needles, salt and pepper to taste and a pinch of sugar, and serve with Chinese pancakes.

If you want to stretch the dish, scramble 2 eggs and add them to it. It tastes good, looks pretty and makes a bigger serving.

Knifemanship

Is using a sharp knife a kitchen secret? If so, it is one of the most important secrets in Chinese cooking. Every Chinese housewife and chef uses a heavy chopper, usually honed to a sharpness that makes a razor look blunt. That is because the way in which ingredients are cut in Chinese cuisine is vital. This is particularly so in Shanghainese dishes where everything is cut into very fine pieces and the meat is often shredded. Sharp knives are an asset in any kitchen, but for Chinese cooking they are especially important.

An awareness of the importance of properly prepared ingredients is something that all good cooks possess. Chinese cooks don't have a monopoly on it. Nor do they have any magic formula known only to themselves. In fact with Chinese cooking — as with any other national cuisine — the choice of the right method of preparation is largely a matter of common sense. Obviously, if you're going to cook the ingredients quickly — as in stir frying — they can't be left in great chunks. Equally obviously, if several ingredients are to be cooked simultaneously and some are 'quicker cookers' than others, you will have to make the necessary allowances. So use the cutting methods indicated in the recipes, with the illustrations on this page as a guide. And use the experience that you have already gained in the kitchen.

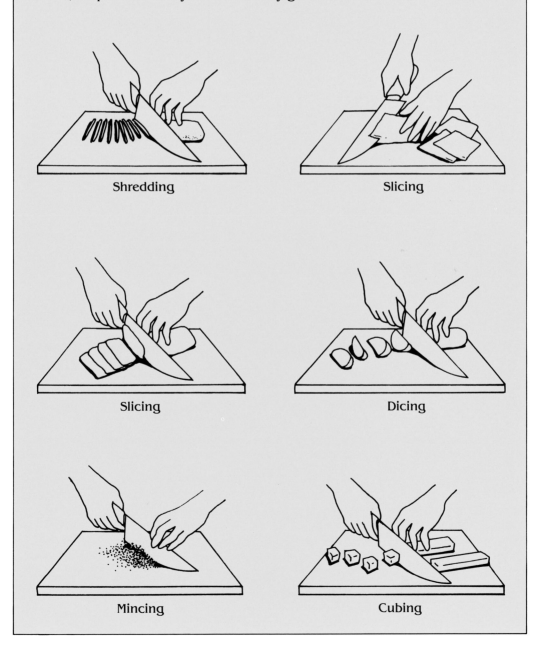

Shredding

Slicing

Slicing

Dicing

Mincing

Cubing

Why? Because Chinese food of all varieties calls for the meat and vegetables to be cut into smaller pieces to enable them to cook through thoroughly and quickly. So, obviously, if you are going to be doing a lot of cutting you want your implements to be in good working order. And knifemanship itself, the degree of skill shown in paring and cutting, is prized in the Chinese kitchen in the same way that the ability to make a good pie crust, for instance, is valued in the West.

When you cut beef for a Chinese dish, you do it in a different way from the manner you would use for a Western stew. In European cuisine, the meat would come off the chopping block in neat cubes. Not so in a Chinese kitchen. Here, the knife or chopper should cut across the grain at an angle, leaving the meat in irregular, angular chunks. It's the same with carrots and other vegetables. Instead of slicing along the length of the vegetables leaving even cubes or circles, you cut at an angle. The result is pieces of food which are unusual shapes with odd angles. In a Chinese dish they look better. They also taste better. Don't ask me why, they just do.

But do not waste all day in the kitchen cutting and slicing your ingredients. A Chinese housewife prepares her vegetables for the wok in a matter of seconds. Just remember to cut on an angle to get interesting and irregular shapes.

Steaming

Steam cooking is probably the least messy form of cooking because while stir frying relies on hot oil, steaming just requires boiling water. Put enough water to reach a depth of about 3 inches in a pot large enough to accommodate what you are cooking. Put the food to be steamed in a bowl or deep plate, and put the bowl or plate inside the pot. The water should already be boiling when you do this to ensure better control over the time for which the food is steamed. Cover the pot with a lid, and let the hot steam do the cooking. At the same time keep an eye on things to make sure that the water doesn't boil off.

STEAMED FISH

Use 1½ to 2 lbs of fish, whole or filleted. Clean the fish and use paper toweling to blot dry. If the fish is whole, score it on both sides.

Salt and pepper both sides of the fish to taste.

Arrange the fish on a plate, sprinkle with 2 tsp of cooking oil, cover generously with shredded ginger and scallion.

Steam for 10 to 15 minutes, then carefully lift up the plate from the.steam pot and serve.

Hint

Steamed fish will not taste good cold, so steam your fish on the same plate that you intend to serve it on. When you use a whole fish, always score it on both sides to ensure that the flavor of the other ingredients gets through. To test if the fish is cooked, use a knife with a sharp point to poke the thickest part of the fish to see if the meat will separate from the bone. The fish is done when the meat is easily parted from the bone. It is important that you only use very fresh fish for steaming. To check the freshness of a fish, look into the gills and poke the eyes. If the gills are red and slimy and the eyes are bulging and look firm, the fish is fresh.

DRUNKEN CHICKEN

Use a whole fryer — about 2½ to 3 lb — or chicken parts. Clean the chicken and use paper toweling to blot dry. Rub salt all over the chicken, inside and outside, and let it stand for about 5 hours (if you are using chicken parts, 4 hours will do).

Place the chicken in a bowl and steam for about 25 minutes.

Remove the chicken from the bowl and let it cool. If you are using a whole chicken, cut it into 6 to 8 pieces. Put the chicken pieces or parts into a container that can be covered. Add 1½ to 2 cups of dry white wine, Chinese Shao Hsing wine or dry sherry and the chicken broth from the bowl in which the chicken was steamed (there is bound to be some broth left over after the steaming process). Cover and leave in the refrigerator for a day. Turn the chicken a couple of times during the marinating process to make sure that it gets 'drunk' all over.

Take the chicken parts out of the wine, cut them into 1-inch to 2-inch pieces and lay them nicely on the serving plate.

SOY SAUCE FISH — RED COOKED FISH

Use 1½ to 2 lbs of fish, whole or filleted. Clean the fish and use paper toweling to blot dry. If the fish is whole, score it on both sides, if it is filleted, cut the fillets into bite-sized pieces.

Salt and pepper the fish on both sides and dust lightly with corn-starch or flour. (This is to prevent the skin of a whole fish from getting stuck to the frying pan, and to act as a binder to keep fish fillet pieces from falling apart when cooking.

Heat ½ cup of oil in a frying pan, add the fish and brown it on both sides.

Add ½ cup of chopped ginger, scallion and celery, mixed together in equal proportions, and 2 to 3 tbsp each of wine or water and soy sauce. Reduce the heat to low, cover the frying pan with a lid and simmer the fish for 3 to 5 minutes. Turn the fish over, simmer again for another 2 to 3 minutes, add a pinch of sugar and serve.

Hint
When the fish is simmering, make sure that there is enough liquid in the pan. If there isn't, add more wine or cold water.

STEAMED EGG-PLANTS

Cut 2 egg-plants lengthways into quarters and steam for 20 minutes until soft.

Do you have a favorite salad dressing that is not cream or milk based?

Just add to it 1 or 2 cloves of garlic (crushed) — depending on how much you like raw garlic — ½ tsp soy sauce, 1 tsp sesame oil and a dash of sugar. Shake the mixture well and pour it over the cooled egg-plant. This is a favored summer dish of the Northern Chinese.

PLAIN STEAMED CHICKEN

Use the same ingredients and method as for Drunken Chicken, but omit the wine. When the chicken is cooked, take it from the bowl and put it on your chopping board. Let it cool for a few minutes, then chop it, bones and all, into small pieces. Serve with a scallion and ginger sauce as a dip. To make the sauce, mix 1 tbsp each of grated ginger and scallion in a small bowl. Heat 3 to 4 tbsp of cooking oil and when it is smoking hot, pour it into the bowl. That's the sauce for the waiting bird.

STEAMED BEAN CURD WITH MINCED PORK OR MINCED CHICKEN OR TURKEY

Rinse 3 squares of bean curd under cold water, slice into smaller squares, salt and pepper to taste, and put in a bowl or a deep plate.

Mix ½ lb of minced meat with a stalk of scallion (chopped) and 2 slices of ginger root (minced) or a pinch of ginger powder, 1 tsp soy sauce, a dash of pepper and a pinch of sugar. Mix the ingredients well, then spread or dot the minced meat on top of the bean curd. Steam for 12 to 15 minutes and serve in the same bowl or plate.

STEAMED EGG CUSTARD WITH SHRIMP

Lightly beat 4 eggs in a bowl. Mix in 1½ cups of water or chicken stock and salt and pepper to taste (you may use soy sauce instead of salt).

Clean and devein 1 lb of shrimp, use paper toweling to blot dry, then arrange in the egg mix and dot with a little finely chopped scallion.

Place the bowl in a steamer or pot and steam over high heat for 2 minutes. Reduce the heat to medium and continue to steam for another 20 minutes until the custard is firm. Serve in the same bowl.

Hint
When serving, sprinkle 1 tsp of wine vinegar on top of the custard. It produces a delicate taste. You can omit the shrimp to make a plain egg custard, or replace the shrimp with minced clams, crab meat, lightly minced pork, minced chicken, etc. The plain egg custard is a comforting and nutritious dish for anyone suffering from a sore throat.

Stretching what you've got

Imagine you want to whip up a quick meal for the family at the end of a long weekend and the larder is getting bare. You don't have enough to feed them steak, Western style, because you only have two in the freezer. But that is more than enough for a Chinese beef dish for eight people. Or you've got half a cooked chicken. There is the basis for another dish. The beauty of Chinese food is that you can take what ingredients you have, chop up a few vegetables and, hey presto!, you've produced a marvelous Chinese family meal.

Those not in the know will think you are a genius. They will not know how simple it is. Don't tell them. Let them think you are an Asian Escoffier. That's another beauty of Chinese home cooking; you can take a little and make it go a very long way.

TEXTURE AND TASTE

The humble sea slug is not the most beautiful of God's creatures. But it is a favored item in many a Chinese kitchen because it has one elusive quality that is hard to find; texture. The slug has no taste. It has to be cooked with a generous amount of crab meat or fish roe because by itself it is outstanding only for its blandness. But it has a chewy, digestible texture, an indefinable quality. So does the jellyfish. Now, I am not suggesting that you should rush out and obtain sea slugs, jellyfish and other unattractive creatures and attempt to cook them. I am trying to show that in addition to appearance, aroma and taste, the combinations of texture are also a consideration in Chinese cooking.

I must confess that after 30 years in Asia, my husband still blanches when he sees a sea slug or a bowl of jellyfish approaching the table. He does not appreciate the Chinese admiration for their unique texture.

Egg foo into a new dish

The egg is a marvelous thing. Foreigners visiting the East love to wander through back street markets and look at the huge cane baskets of what are known as hundred year eggs, covered with a thick black coating of indescribable dirt and inside containing an egg of green and evil hue. Forget them. Think of the eggs in your kitchen and what you can do with them. You can do a lot.

The wonder of the egg is that it is a catalyst that can make simple things so elegant. It is a gift from nature that allows you to take a bit of this and a handful of that and a cupful of the other and produce something wonderful, something elusive like the alchemists of old used to seek, something that is bigger than all its parts.

Let me explain what I mean.

You are at home with the children and don't feel like cooking. Or you come home tired after a long day and want to get dinner

Egg with Shallots & Chilli Peppers; Egg with Shredded Pork & Scallions; Egg with Sliced Beef

over and done with. What are you going to do? You rummage through the kitchen. You've got a few scraps of pork from last night's dinner. You've got some frozen peas. You've got some scallions. You've got the makings of a magnificent dish!

And the possible combinations? They are limitless.

THE MASTER RECIPE FOR EGG FOO YUNG ANYTHING

Egg foo yung dishes are among the easiest to cook, offer a great opportunity for creativity and make for a good, quick lunch. Foo yung sounds very mysterious. It means to beautify, and egg foo yung is simply an effort to descriptively dress up scrambled eggs with either crab meat, shrimp, beef, pork, chicken, scallions, onion, tomatoes, bean sprouts, bean curd, hot pepper, green pepper, garlic or a combination of several of these ingredients.

Follow the stir fry method to cook about 1 cup of a mixture of ingredients that sounds most tasty to you. Scoop the cooked mixture out of the pan.

Beat 4 to 5 eggs, depending on the size of the eggs, mix in the stir fried ingredients, and salt and pepper to taste.

Heat 2 to 3 tbsp of oil, add the mixture of egg and stir fried ingredients and scramble. When the eggs are no longer loose, scoop the mixture out of the pan and serve.

Hint
Any foo yung dish is a good base for fried rice. Canned crab or shrimp are fine for a foo yung dish, and you can even try canned clam — drained and minced. Of course, any left-over stir fried dishes can be the base for foo yung dishes. In fact that's probably how it all started.

A living cuisine

Chinese family cooking is a living cuisine. It does not exist in a vacuum and like everything else is affected by its environment. Look at Shanghainese food in Hong Kong. The people who go to Shanghainese restaurants are often second generation Hong Kong residents. They have eaten Cantonese food most of their lives. The chefs are probably Cantonese. The Shanghainese dishes they eat are probably going to have a Cantonese flavor.

It's the same with Chinese food overseas. In America, it will appeal to American tastes. In Britain, it will have an indefinable British flavor. In Denmark, many years ago, a side order of potatoes was put before me in a Chinese restaurant. Then there is the international Chinese cuisine such as the immortal (or immoral!) canned chop suey. For goodness' sake. I would like to meet the man who thought of this. I hope he isn't Chinese.

Cold dishes

Here are six cold dishes which are easy to prepare and can be done well in advance of your dinner, making it possible for you to spend more time with your guests when you serve Chinese food.

SWEET AND SOUR CABBAGE WITH DRY RED PEPPER

Clean about 2 lb of cabbage or Chinese cabbage and cut or tear it into large pieces as you would do with lettuce when making a salad.

Cut 4 to 6 dried red peppers into 1-inch strips. The seeds in red peppers are particularly hot, so if you like it hot, don't remove them. (You can substitute 1½ tsp of red pepper flakes.)

Heat ¼ cup of oil in a frying pan, add the hot pepper strips and stir fry them until they turn dark, then add 15 to 20 brown peppercorns and the cabbage and stir fry quickly over very high heat for 2 minutes.

Add 2 tbsp each of soy sauce, sugar and vinegar, and 2 tsp of salt, and stir fry for another ¼ to 1 minute. Just before scooping the mixture onto a plate, sprinkle ½ tsp of sesame oil over it.

Allow the dish to cool to room temperature, or refrigerate it. It tastes better when cold.

SICHUAN CUCUMBER

Cut 6 to 7 small cucumbers into diagonal strips, sprinkle them with 1 tsp of salt, and let them sit for 1 to 2 hours in a bowl.

Rinse the cucumber strips with cold water, use paper toweling to blot dry and put back in the bowl.

Add 4 cloves of garlic (crushed), 15 to 20 brown peppercorns, 2 tsp each of red pepper oil and sesame oil, 1 tsp vinegar and 2 tsp sugar. Mix and leave to stand for 2 hours. Then refrigerate to serve cold as pickles.

Kept in the refrigerator it will be good for a week. Use a tight cover to keep the garlic from smelling up the refrigerator.

The brown peppercorns are from a pungent wild pepper that grows in Western China and are not commonly used in Western cooking. The combination of red chilli and brown peppercorns gives Sichuan food a taste which is distinctive from the rest of Chinese cooking. The brown peppercorns are called Hwa Jao and can be found in Chinese grocery stores along with the Five Spices and star anise, both of which are often used in stews. I am personally very fond of Sichuan cooking, having spent my childhood years in that region during the last world war. I like it hot.

BEAN CURD

If a Chinese man is described as someone who likes to eat bean curd, it's likely that the description carries the slang meaning that he's fond of teasing girls. But let's dismiss this sexist approach and deal with the real thing. Bean curd.

If you are into health food, bean curd is the thing for you. It's loaded with protein and you can be sure it's clean, since it won't curdle if it's dirty.

Here is one of the most simple bean curd dishes of all. Take 2 or 3 cubes of bean curd (it usually comes in cubes), rinse in cold water and slice into smaller cubes. Put 1 or 2 stalks of scallions (chopped) on top of the bean curd. Mix salt, pepper and soy sauce with the bean curd to taste, and sprinkle with a little sesame oil before serving. A good summer cold dish.

Here is another easy one. Shred or cut cucumber into small pieces, salt and pepper and mix with the above seasoned bean curd. Call it cucumber salad with bean curd dressing and serve it as a salad with your Western roast chicken dinner. You will probably receive a lot of oohs and ahs.

SHAO HSING WINE

Most Shanghainese dishes call for wine. Don't go out of your way to buy the special Shao Hsing wine which, in addition to being a good drinking wine, is the most common variety used in Shanghai cooking. Use sherry or common white wine instead — the wine you use in the everyday cooking of Western dishes.

BON BON CHICKEN

Boil 2 chicken breasts (medium-sized to large) for about 25 minutes in water to which salt, pepper, a stalk of scallion and slice of ginger root has been added. Take out the chicken breasts, allow them to cool, and shred them.

Shred 2 to 3 small cucumbers (if the skin is not tough, leave it on, it has a wonderful flavor and color). Arrange the shredded cucumber around the shredded chicken on a plate.

Mix 2 tbsp of sesame paste (if not available, mix 2 tsp each of creamy peanut butter and sesame oil as a substitute), 1½ tsp of soy sauce, 1 or more tsp of chilli oil, 1 clove of garlic (crushed), salt and pepper to taste, a pinch of sugar, and 2 crushed roasted brown peppers, if you have them. Keep the chicken and cucumber and the sauce in the refrigerator. When you are ready to serve, just pour the sauce over the chicken and cucumber.

FIVE FLAVORED BEEF

Following the basic method, stew a 1 lb piece of beef shin or pot roast beef with such spices as ginger, scallion, soy sauce, pepper, etc. Add 1 tsp of five fragrant powder or 2 pieces of star anise and cook and simmer for 1 hour. Cool and cut into thin slices, and arrange on a plate. You can leave it at room temperature or refrigerate it, depending on when you intend to serve. Just before serving, sprinkle with some chopped scallion for color and a little sesame oil for flavor.

*The Buddha Jumps over the Temple Wall; The Lion's Head;
Pock-Faced Old Lady's Bean Curd; Ants on the Tree*

PORK WITH GARLIC SAUCE

This is a dish for the garlic lover. If you hate garlic, then skip it.

Boil 1 lb of pork loin or shoulder for 40 minutes in water together with a little salt and pepper, a stalk of scallion and a slice of ginger root or a pinch of ginger powder.

When the pork is cooked, allow it to cool, cut it into very thin slices, and arrange the slices on a plate. You can leave it at room temperature or refrigerate it.

Mix 1 tsp each of vinegar, sugar, sesame oil and chilli oil (or pepper flakes), 1 tbsp of soy sauce, a pinch of salt and 5 or 6 cloves of garlic (finely crushed). Cook the mixture in 1 tbsp of oil for 2 minutes. Cook, taste, and pour the sauce over the sliced pork.

If you have any special Sichuan brown peppers, roast a couple, crush them and sprinkle into the sauce mixture. You can add more of any of the ingredients to adjust the flavor, but remember it should be garlicky and spicy hot.

Five Flavored Beef; Pork with Garlic Sauce; Bon Bon Chicken

Dishes with picturesque names

The Chinese language can be flowery and colorful at times. Ask your Chinese friends about the literal meaning of their given Chinese names. From the women, you'll get a lot of very precious jades, elegant virtues, beautiful orchids and the like. From the men, you'll get hordes of brave warriors, diligent scholars, national saviors and so on. This linguistic extravagance is also evident in Chinese foods. There is one dish, for example, which bears the name 'The Buddha jumps over the Temple Wall'. I won't go into the recipe — it's somewhat complicated — but it's really nothing more than a stew. The name derives from the supposition that the stew is so tasty and fragrant that if Buddha had been around to smell it, he would have abandoned his meditations and leaped over the temple wall to get at the dish. Other colorfully-named and easy-to-make dishes are as follows.

THE LION'S HEAD

These are really giant-sized ½ lb meat balls with a Chinese twist. To make 4 lion's heads, use 2 lbs of ground pork. (You can use other ground meat or a mixture of ground meats, as some people do with their meat loafs, but the traditional lion's head uses ground pork only.) Since this is a Shanghai dish, we have to use wine, soy sauce and more than just a pinch of sugar. Add to the ground meat 4 to 5 tsp of soy sauce, 2 slices of ginger root (minced), 2 stalks of scallion (finely chopped), 5 or 6 water chestnuts (finely chopped) — if you don't have fresh ones, canned ones will do — 1 tsp of wine, 2 tsp of cornstarch, 1 tsp of sugar and 2 eggs. Mix the ingredients together very well — the more you mix, the softer the meat balls will be. Make 4 equal sized meat balls — if you find the meat is too loose to form into balls, add more cornstarch or flour.

Heat 5 or 6 tsp of oil in a pan, brown the meat balls on all sides. When browned, pour in a mixture of 1 cup of chicken broth (or water) and 3 tsp of dry sherry or Shao Hsing wine. Bring the mixture to the boil, reduce the heat, cover and simmer for 30 minutes. While simmering, turn the meat once. Take the meat balls out of the simmering sauce, lay half a Chinese cabbage (cut into quarters) at the bottom of the pot, salt and pepper a little, then put back the meat balls. Bring the sauce to the boil, reduce the heat, cover and simmer for another 20 to 30 minutes.

ANTS ON THE TREE

This is a stir fried dish of minced pork (the ants) and bean noodles (the twigs of a tree). In place of pork you can use minced beef, chicken or turkey. It's a Sichuan specialty, so it should be on the hot and spicy side.

Sauté ginger, scallion and garlic in oil, add about ½ lb of minced meat, ½ tsp (less or more depending on how hot you want it) of chilli flakes, and soy and pepper to taste. Stir fry until the meat is well done, then add 2 cups of pre-soaked and drained bean noodles. Mix together with the meat and stir until the noodles are hot. Add a pinch of sugar and serve.

POCK · FACED OLD LADY'S BEAN CURD

This is a simple Sichuan stir fried dish made of minced pork with bean curd. Supposedly during World War II there was a pock-faced old lady in Chungking who ran a hole-in-a-wall eating place where she cooked this simply fantastic dish. Later on, any restaurant serving the dish would claim to have gotten the secret recipe from her.

Stir fry the minced pork in the same way, and with the same ingredients, as with Ants on the Tree. Add 3 squares of bean curd cut into smaller cubes. Stir fry together for 1 minute or more to allow the bean curd to get hot and soak up some flavor from the meat, then taste, add a pinch of sugar and serve.

Whenever you cook a Sichuan dish, if you have brown pepper in the house, roast a few in the pan and crush them into flakes to use with the hot chilli pepper flakes in the dish.

PEEPING IS ALLOWED

There is a school of thought that insists that you should never lift the lid of a steamer while a dish is cooking. Why on earth not? What have you got to lose except a little bit of steam which will be replaced in a few seconds once you put the lid back on. If you are cooking a Drunken Chicken and want to see if the bird is done, by all means open the steamer and poke a skewer into the flesh to see if it is cooked. The chicken is not going to fly away. It's the same with fish. Test it to see if it is cooked. The carp is not going to swim anywhere.

The miraculous bean

It is said that man cannot live by bread alone. He can, however, live by bean alone — especially if it is that miracle of nature the soya bean.

This humble legume has been cultivated in China for at least 5,000 years. It was around when China's ancient history began. There are at least 2,500 varieties and the beans come in every size, shape and color. The plants are easy to grow and give an enormous yield per acre. In one form or another, the plant provides almost everything needed for a healthy diet.

Westerners are probably most familiar with it as a sauce or flavoring. It is also used as a vegetable oil, as a high-quality flour, a milk-like drink packed with protein, as curds and cake and as a coffee substitute. The green crop is used as forage for grazing stock and provides hay for animal winter feed. Pressed into huge wheels, it is a valuable fertiliser. It is used to make industrial

How to make Soy Milk

products as diverse as printer's ink and plastics and a substitute for rubber. All in all, a most valuable plant.

But what concerns us is the curd known as tou fu. It comes in many forms, all of which provide the basis of a healthy diet. You can fry it, you can use it in soups, you can braise it with meat and you can add sugar and eat it as a sweet. No matter what you do with it, tou fu will do you good. In Northern China, where it originated, it is verily the staff of life. It is cheaper than meat and a lot healthier.

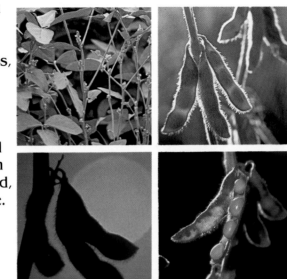

Stuffed Fried Bean Curd Puffs;
Bean Curd Family Style;
Pressed Dry Bean Curd with Beef

Tou fu in some of its myriad forms is now being sold around the world. In Western countries, it can be bought not only in health food stores and Chinatown grocery stores, but increasingly in supermarkets. The West is learning what the East knew 50 centuries ago — tou fu is good for you. It is also incredibly useful in Chinese family cooking because it forms the basis for many nourishing vegetable meals in which it is used as a meat substitute. Tou fu, depending on how it is prepared, has a variety of flavors. It also picks up the flavors of the vegetables, meats and sauces with which it is cooked.

HOW TO MAKE SOY MILK

This is an excellent milk substitute, a health food drink and a vegetarian's delight.

Soak 1 cup of dried soy beans in 2 cups of cold water overnight.

Mix the soaked soy beans with 4 cups of fresh water and liquify it in a blender.

Strain the liquid into a cooking pot through a piece of cheese-cloth or a dish cloth, squeezing to get all the soy milk out.

Bring the soy milk to a slow boil over medium to low heat, and boil for 2 minutes. Do not cover the pot with a lid.

Add sugar. You can drink the milk hot, or refrigerate it and drink it cold. It will keep for 3 days under refrigeration.

Hint

You can also make a soup by adding salt, pepper, soy sauce, chopped scallion, and a few drops of sesame oil or hot oil, to taste. Sprinkling a little vinegar in your soup bowl will make the soy milk curdle into a thick soup. Try it — it's kitchen chemistry.

STUFFED FRIED BEAN CURD PUFFS

Use about ½ lb of minced pork prepared in the same way as lion's head meatballs. Slit open 18 bean curd puffs and stuff with the minced pork. Stir fry the stuffed puffs in oil with a bit of ginger and scallion for about 1 minute, add ¼ to ⅓ cup of water and simmer for 15 minutes to ensure that the meat stuffing is cooked, then scoop the puffs out. There should be some liquid left in the pan. If not, add a little water and stir in soy sauce, 1 tsp of cornstarch and a pinch of sugar to make a small amount of gravy to pour over the puffs. Don't forget to taste before serving. If you want to have vegetables in this dish, you can add 2 cups of Chinese cabbage, or regular cabbage, right after you put the ginger and scallions in the pan.

Note

If you don't have bean puffs available, forget them and just make small meat balls and cook them with cabbage in the same way. If you like it a bit chilli hot, add pepper flakes. Incidentally, keep in mind that all forms of bean curd have already been processed and are edible without cooking.

PRESSED DRY BEAN CURD WITH BEEF

Stir fry ½ lb of shredded beef with a touch of ginger and chopped scallion in oil for 30 seconds, then scoop the meat out.

Add oil to the same pan, stir fry some sliced pressed dry bean curd (a common commodity in Chinese groceries) and salt and pepper to taste. For color as well as flavor, add 1 celery stalk (thinly sliced) or 1 green pepper (sliced). Stir for 30 seconds or a little longer.

Put the beef back into the pan and stir fry everything together for 30 seconds. Add a pinch of sugar, taste and serve.

BEAN CURD FAMILY STYLE

Slice 3 squares of bean curd into eighths. Heat ¼ cup of oil and fry a few pieces of the bean curd at a time on both sides until brown, and salt to taste. As you fry the remainder, add more oil if need be. Put the browned bean curd on a plate. Use the remaining hot oil to stir fry for about 30 seconds 3 or 4 stalks of scallions cut into 3-inch lengths, a handful of fresh mushrooms or pre-soaked black mushrooms, and ¼ cup of sliced bamboo shoots. Add salt and pepper to taste. Put the fried bean curd back into the pan and mix and stir for 1 minute. Sprinkle with a little soy sauce to give some color, and add a pinch of sugar.

The yin and the yang

The Chinese belief in the balances of life — the yin and the yang, female and male, dark and light — extends into the kitchen and onto the table. Some foods are held to be hot, others cold.

Peppers, of course, are hot. So are oranges. Watermelons, obviously, are cold. So are most fish and seafood (lobster is the exception).

Chinese tradition has it that if you eat too much 'hot' food (hot in the sense of the inherent quality, not in terms of temperature or pepper) you will break out in sores. Hot foods are fried or oily. Cold foods are water plants and crabs. Green beans are cold. Red beans are hot. Chinese housewives have believed for centuries that 'hot' and 'cold' foods should be served in every meal. As with everything else in life, they believe in a dietary balance between the yin and the yang.

Can you use a microwave oven for Chinese cooking?

If you cook the same Chinese dish a number of times using exactly the same ingredients, the taste will be slightly different every time because, as you remember, the intensity of the heat is a very important factor. Don't worry too much about this — the brighter side is that you'll never have a complete failure as you might have with a cake or soufflé.

However the ever-increasingly popular microwave method of cooking is not much of a help in Chinese cuisine. It's not made for stir frying or stewing although you can, of course, use it to heat foods, and you can also use it to approximate the steaming process.

You can do steamed fish or chicken this way. Prepare the food as you would for regular steaming, cover it with Saran wrap and put it directly into the mircowave oven (no steamer or water is used). Try doing the fish for about 10 to 12 minutes, or figure out a rough time according to the microwave oven instructions. A rough guide for a chicken (2½ to 3 lbs) is 30 minutes — drunk or sober.

Noodles

Noodles are a common dish throughout China, and they are also
a must for birthdays. This is because noodles are long and are
therefore regarded as a symbol of long life. The noodle dish I'm
now going to tell you about is a Northern Chinese equivalent of a
birthday cake. For all we know, this may be the dish which
inspired Marco Polo to bring back noodles to Italy where they
were transformed into spaghetti.

CHIA CHIANG MEIN

Sauté some chopped scallion and ginger in 2 tbsp of oil, add 1 lb
of finely cubed or minced pork or beef, and stir fry until the pork
or beef is well done.

Add ½ cup each of Hoisin sauce, soy bean paste (you can readily
buy both of these in Chinese groceries) and water. Bring the
mixture to a slow boil, cover the pot with a lid and simmer for 30
to 40 minutes over low heat. Stir the sauce frequently to prevent
it from sticking and burning. The texture and thickness of the
sauce should be similar to that of spaghetti sauce.

Boil a pot of water and blanch some spinach, bean sprouts and chives. Cut the spinach and chives into 2-inch lengths and arrange on a plate together with the bean sprouts and some raw shredded cucumber.

Boil enough noodles (spaghetti is fine) for about 4 or 5 people. When cooked, divide into portions to fill 4 or 5 large bowls. Put the sauce and the blanched vegetables on a platter, and — as with the meat sauce for spaghetti — let each person decide on how much sauce to use with the noodles. The blanched vegetables are the equivalent of salad, but instead of being eaten separately, they are added to the noodles and the sauce. After you've achieved a mix you like, sprinkle in 1 tsp of vinegar to give the dish a delicate flavor. In Northern China, this dish is commonly accompanied by raw garlic cloves which are nibbled as the noodles are eaten. This is a strong experience! If you like garlic, you can add a raw clove to the noodles in the bowl. In this way, you'll get some of the flavor without being obliged to eat the garlic.

Chia Chiang Mein (Noodle)

Stewing

It may seem a little incongruous, but to make a rich and hearty Chinese family stew, you start off with the stir frying technique. Like everything else about Chinese food, it's simple. You begin with oil in your wok or pot and braise the meat or chicken to get it brown in exactly the same way as you do for a Western stew. Then you add water and soy, put the lid on the pot and leave the mixture to simmer. Check it occasionally to see how things are progressing, add more soy or salt or pepper as called for and put in the vegetables at the appropriate times (10 minutes for hard vegetables like potatoes, 5 for beans). At the last second add a handful of scallions to give the mixture color as well as taste. You can also use more exotic herbs and spices like anise pepper, cassia, cinnamon bark, cloves or fennel, in the same way as you do in Western stews.

Now, is that complicated?

Stewed Duck with Black Mushrooms

STEWED DUCK

First clean the duck thoroughly (a good way is to plunge it into boiling water for a few minutes) and rinse well.

Put 2 stalks of scallion, 3 or 4 thick slices of ginger root, ½ cup each of soy sauce, wine and water and some pepper in a pot. Bring the mixture to the boil and add the duck. Continue with high heat until the sauce returns to the boil, then reduce the heat, cover the pot with a lid and simmer or stew for about 1 hour or a little longer, until the duck is soft. During the simmering, baste the duck and also turn it over once to get both sides immersed in the sauce. After about ½ hour of simmering, add about 15 large black mushrooms which have been soaked in water. Keep the water in which the mushrooms were soaked — it has a good strong flavor, and if you discover that the sauce in the pot is running low, add some mushroom water to keep the duck from getting too dry or burned. To see if the duck is done, poke the meaty part with a fork. If the fork goes through easily, you're all set. Take the duck out carefully to avoid having it fall apart, put it on the serving dish and arrange the mushrooms around it. Taste the sauce, season to taste, add a pinch of sugar, and perhaps some cornstarch to thicken it. Pour it over the duck and serve.

STEWED CHICKEN WITH CHESTNUT, STEWED CHICKEN WITH GOLDEN NEEDLE, STEWED BEEF WITH WHITE TURNIP, STEWED LAMB WITH SHALLOTS

For these four dishes, follow the general instructions for stewing. After sautéing and browning the meat with ginger and scallion, add 1 tbsp of soy sauce per 1 lb of meat. Mix the meat and the soy

CHOPSTICKS

What came first, chopsticks or the Chinese method of cooking food in bite-sized pieces? It's like the old question of the chicken and the egg. Nobody knows the answer. But no matter what the schedule is, there is no doubt that chopsticks are the perfect instruments for eating Chinese food. They are also a great cooking aid. You can pluck a piece of food from the hot wok to taste with no danger of burning your fingers or your tongue. You can stir stews and soup. Chopsticks come in handy for a multitude of uses. I couldn't do without them and I suggest you buy yourself a bundle because they are also useful implements to use in Western cooking. Do not waste your money buying the expensive ivory type, though. The plain wooden chopsticks do the job.

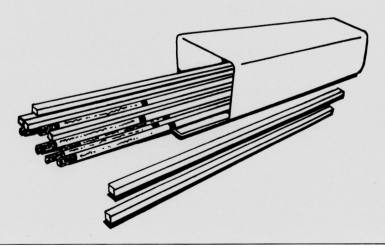

sauce thoroughly together — in addition to its salty flavor, the soy sauce gives the brown color characteristic of Chinese stews. Add ⅓ to ½ cup of water per 1 lb of meat, and you can add some wine if you like. Bring to the boil, reduce the heat, cover the pot with a lid and stew. A 2 to 2½ lb chicken will take about 45 minutes. Beef, lamb, or pork will take about 1 hour or more. When you cook Chinese stew the first time, check periodically to get the feel of how the meat is doing, and how different meats react to the amount of liquid you use. Make little adjustments by adding more soy sauce — or more water, if you feel that the flavor is too strong. Before you serve, add a bit of sugar or rock sugar. If the gravy is not thick enough for your liking, add a little cornstarch.

Note
Soak the dry vegetables and add them about 15 minutes before the stew is done. This is enough time for them to soak up the flavor of the sauce.

Stewed Chicken with Chestnut; Stewed Chicken with Golden Needle

Insulting yourself

People sometimes ask me how they should cook fried rice for a dinner. The answer is simple. You shouldn't. To serve your guests fried rice is an insult. An insult to yourself. Don't get me wrong. I love fried rice. I serve it all the time. But not as a dish in itself. Fried rice is a left-over dish. It's a makeshift hotch-potch of anything you can find during a search of your refrigerator. It's something to throw together for yourself and your family or *very* close friends in an extremely informal way. But if you are cooking a Chinese meal, fried rice should *never* be on the menu. Why? Well, in the Western context, if you had invited friends for a meal would you feed them left-overs? Probably not, and that's what fried rice is — a warmed-up collection of left-overs, rather like the English bubble-and-squeak. I like that, too, but I would raise an eyebrow if I was invited into a friend's home in London and found it on the table.

Rice

Estimates vary, but some agronomists believe there are more than 7,000 varieties of rice grown in China. We need concern ourselves only with two main strains, the short-grained and the long-grained rice which can be bought in any supermarket in America. If you don't have a rice cooker, the best way to prepare rice to accompany your home-cooked Chinese meal is in a simple pot.

Rice occupies a unique place in Chinese life. In Chinese, the very description of eating means to 'take rice'. And if you are a public servant with a secure job, you are said to have an 'iron ice bowl', meaning that you will never be hungry because your rice bowl cannot be broken since it is very rare for bureaucrats to be sacked.

HOW TO COOK RICE

For rice lovers, I strongly recommend that you buy an electric rice cooker. Hong Kong, Taiwan and Japan all make good ones with different sizes to suit your family needs. If you only eat rice occasionally, though, here is the way to cook it — keeping in mind that 1 cup of uncooked rice will produce twice the amount of cooked rice.

Wash and drain the rice.

Place in an uncovered saucepan and add 1¼ cups of water for every cup of rice.   Bring rapidly to the boil.

Reduce the heat to medium and keep boiling until most of the water is boiled off. This should take about 3 to 5 minutes.

Reduce the heat to very low, cover the saucepan and cook for about another 15 to 20 minutes. For a larger amount of rice — 5 cups or more — 30 minutes might be needed. Experiment a couple of times — you'll quickly get the hang of it.

Use a fork or a pair of chopsticks to fluff the rice before serving. If left covered in the saucepan on the warm stove, the rice will keep hot for at least half an hour.

HOW TO COOK FRIED RICE

Cooking fried rice is a very simple matter. With the exception of fish and sweet and sour dishes, you can use any left-over stir fried dish to mix with cold cooked rice to make a simple yet tasty meal that goes well with a cup of coffee or tea.

Sauté a little chopped onion or scallion in 2 tsp of oil. When brown, mix in about 2 cups of cooked cold rice and your left-over dish. There are no exact proportions. You all know what fried rice looks like — and anyway make the mix to your own taste. One variation is to scramble 2 eggs with chopped scallion, mix in cold rice and stir fry until hot. This in itself is a popular fried rice dish, but you can always combine it with left-overs. Do the eggs first, then mix in the rice and the left-overs. However, you needn't confine yourself to left-overs for this dish. You can start by stir frying a dish and when it's done, put it aside on a plate. Then use the same frying pan to heat the cold rice, plop the dish you've just made back into the pan with the rice, mix until it's all hot, and serve.

Hint
Don't throw the cold rice into the just completed stir fried dish. It takes time to get cold rice hot, and by then your stir fried meat and vegetables will be overcooked and not so tasty.

Don't use just cooked hot rice to make fried rice because it tends to become sticky. Room temperature or refrigerated rice is fine.

Peking duck

If you told the average American or European housewife that you wanted her to cook Peking Duck, she would probably faint. She shouldn't because, as with so many aspects of Chinese food, the mystery that surrounds Peking Duck is needless. In fact, preparing a home-made version of the best-known dish of Northern China is so easy that anyone can do it.

Peking Duck is famous for its crispy skin. In the past, ducks to be

used for the dish were force-fed and confined to a small area to prevent them getting enough exercise to burn off calories. Air would be pumped under the skin of the dressed and cleaned bird to dry the skin and separate it from the fat just beneath it. The duck would then be hung outside for a few hours to dry in the autumn breeze. Traditionally, Peking Duck was eaten only in the autumn. In the summer, the duck would spoil in the heat, while in the winter it would freeze. But the dry autumn breeze was perfect.

Peking Lamb; Peking Beef; Peking Chicken

Now you are obviously not going to hang ducks up around your house — and even if you did, the chances are that the climate wouldn't be right. Don't worry though. You can still make the dish without any problem and surprise your family. I can assure you that the Peking Duck you get in restaurants is not a product of the traditional method. Instead someone has taken a short cut similar to the one that I'm suggesting.

My recipe for Peking Duck is simple.

Clean the duck thoroughly, inside and outside, and use paper toweling to blot the skin dry. Slightly salt and oil the skin, and roast the duck in a pre-heated oven at 325 to 350 degrees for about 20 minutes per pound, making sure that you get the skin really crisp.

After removing the duck from the oven, let it cool for a while. Then go about the slicing — a very important part of the Peking Duck process. You should first try to cut off thin slices of the skin. (In the old days, little was eaten but the skin, but who can afford that now.) Follow your surgery on the skin by slicing off the meat. Finally, put the bones into a pot to make a soup later on.

Unlike most of the recipes in this book, Peking Duck does require a special ingredient. This is the plum sauce — half sweet, half tart — that is the traditional accompaniment.

Once you have your roast duck and your plum sauce, all you need are some scallions, cut into 3-inch lengths, and a stack of magic pancakes. Take a pancake, put a slice or two of skin and/or meat on it, add a couple of pieces of scallion, dipped liberally in the plum sauce, then roll up the pancake, pick it up in your fingers and enjoy the prince of Northern Chinese dishes.

Now, does that sound difficult? Of course not, but the mystique that has grown up around Peking Duck makes one think that to cook the dish is a scientific and culinary marvel. Nothing could be further from the truth, but your friends will not know that. They will be extremely impressed, unless they have read this book themselves. And remember: you can use the same sort of system to cook beef, pork or lamb, served at the table sliced and ready to be wrapped in pancakes. Call these dishes anything you want. No matter what name you give them, they'll be delicious.

Note
You can use Hoisin sauce instead of plum sauce for the dip, and you can easily buy either of them in any Chinese grocery. They come in cans or jars and can be kept for a long time. Once the can or the jar has been opened, store it in a refrigerator.

The magic pancake

Take one part of water and two parts of flour, mix it thoroughly, knead it well and what have you got? The basic ingredient for the magic pancake of Northern China — a thin, flexible piece of dough which can be used in a thousand ways. When I was a girl, I grew up in the kitchen. There was not much to play with so I spent a lot of the time kneading dough. I still do because pancakes with a tasty stuffing make one of my favorite meals. They are also incredibly simple to make.

Once you have the dough thoroughly kneaded, spread some flour on your work surface to prevent sticking. Roll the dough into a long coil and break off small fistfuls. Squeeze these flat with your hand on the table or bench until you have used up all the dough. Oil one side of a patty of dough, by using a brush or dipping the patty into a flat plate with a film of oil.

Take two patties and put the oiled sides together. Roll the joined patties with a rolling pin into a pancake about 5 inches across. Put the pancake into a medium hot pan (experience will soon show you how hot it should be) and turn it over after about 60 seconds. The dough should be lightly browned and bubbles should have appeared. Repeat this with the other side. Now

separate into two pancakes. This should be easy to do because of the film of oil between them.

Now you've got a stack of magic pancakes. When I feel like making pancakes, I make a lot of them. You can wrap them in stacks of 20 or 50 and keep them in your freezer for a year. When you want a genuine Northern Chinese meal, take out as many as you want in the morning, let them thaw, wrap them in aluminium foil and warm them in the oven.

You can fill your pancake with virtually any Chinese dish (or Western food if it comes to that) as long as it is not too runny. You'll find that non-Chinese get a great thrill out of eating the magic pancake. In the north, where bread takes the place of rice, pancakes and buns are everyday food, but for many Westerners who have eaten only Cantonese food, eating Chinese food wrapped in a light but chewy pancake can be a huge amount of fun.

What sort of flour should you use? All-purpose flour for an all-purpose pancake.

Onion Cake

Everyone loves onion cake

This is an old favorite of mine, a dish that can be nibbled as a snack or used as a bread to accompany a meal instead of rice. Make your dough in the same way as for pancakes but when you roll it, make the pancake a bit thicker, about a quarter of an inch. Lightly oil the top of the dough. Add a healthy pinch of salt and spread finely chopped scallions over the top. (You can also put in a little hamburger meat if you have some left-overs.) Roll the pancake into a coil, twist it and flatten it in your hands and then roll it again, this time leaving it about a half-inch thick. Cook the onion cake on both sides for a couple of minutes in a lightly oiled pan or wok over medium heat. Then sprinkle a little water over the cake, cover the pan and let steam for a minute or so. Eat it hot by itself or with any dish. Delicious. And your children will love them.

The last word

Chinese do many things in a different manner to Westerners. Like eating soup. Instead of having their soup at the beginning of a meal, Chinese have it as the last course. Soups in thousands of varieties are believed to aid digestion, therefore they are consumed at the end of a meal. Homemade Chinese soups are usually light and delicate in flavor. Restaurant soups tend to be heavier.

CORN AND CRABMEAT SOUP

This soup is a sure winner and is also very easy to make. Mix 1 can of cream of corn and 1 can of chicken broth (or an equal amount of chicken stock), salt and pepper to taste, and bring the mixture to the boil. Add 1 small can of crab meat, stir a little and bring to a slow boil, adding a little water or chicken stock if the soup is too thick. Turn off the heat, stir in 2 beaten egg whites and serve. This is a good soup to serve as a first course in Western meals, and for variety you can use minced chicken in place of crab meat.

BEAN CURD AND SPINACH SOUP

This is a typical Chinese home style soup and a good calorie-saver for weight-watchers. Use chicken stock or canned chicken broth as the base, slice into the stock 1 or 2 squares of bean curd — depending how much soup you are making — and salt and pepper to taste. Bring to the boil for 1 minute. Cut a couple of handfuls of cleaned, raw spinach into 2-inch or 3-inch lengths. Put the stems into the soup, bring to the boil, then throw in the leaves and immediately turn off the heat. Sprinkle a little finely chopped scallion on top of the soup and serve.

SOUR AND HOT SOUP

This is a very popular Sichuan soup. The pepper used is not red chilli pepper, as with most Sichuan dishes, but white pepper with vinegar. Use about 2 qts of chicken stock or canned chicken broth. Bring to the boil, add 6 medium-sized pre-soaked black mushrooms and ¼ cup each of shredded wood ears, bean curd, canned bamboo shoots and lean pork. Bring back to the boil and add 4 tbsp of vinegar, 1 tbsp of soy sauce, 1½ to 2 tsp of white pepper, 2 tsp of sesame oil and 1 tsp of sugar. Let the soup boil for a couple of minutes and add ½ cup of water or additional broth, mixed with 2 tbsp of cornstarch. Stir the soup, which at this point should be smooth and somewhat thick. Turn off the heat, add 2 slightly beaten eggs, stir once or twice, taste to check the seasoning and serve. It's a good soup for cold weather since the spicy taste will help to keep you warm.

Note
Adjust the amount of white pepper and vinegar to suit your own taste. I suggest that you go easy on them at first since you can add more before serving, if you feel that the soup is too bland.

Bridal soup

Superstitions and traditions about food permeate Chinese life. Some of them are charming, like the special soup prepared for a bride on her wedding night. It is a thick, sweet soup and contains many ingredients such as prunes and lotus seeds and many other morsels. But it is not the taste of the ingredients that matters. It is, rather, the way they sound. Translated, the names of the ingredients can also mean such things as 'many sons', 'early sons', '100 years togetherness' and 'robustly complete'.

Together, they make up a propitious sound which wishes the couple a long and happy life together, with many male children.

Bridal Soup

Mongolian BBQ

You have all heard of tartar steak or, more fancifully, steak tartare. Do you know the origin? Well, a Tartar is a Mongol. You'll find history books referring variously to the Mongol or Tartar hordes of Ghenghis Khan. Actually, there weren't any hordes as the Mongols, then as now, were relatively small in number. But they appeared to the frightened Europeans as hordes because of their incredible mobility by 13th century standards, resulting from their fine horsemanship and endurance. Instead of taking time for a lunch break, they would often put a piece of raw meat under their saddles. The constant jolting from the ride would tenderize the meat which then would be eaten raw, on the move.

Not everything the Mongols ate was raw, though. One of their favoured forms of cooking was over a grill — something similar to what many of you indulge in on a summer Sunday afternoon in the back yard. However there are differences. In Northern China we eat Mongolian BBQ outdoors in late autumn or early winter with everyone bundled up in bulky sweaters and padded jackets. Fiery White Lightning or Mao Tai whisky accompanies the food as an anti-freeze.

Again the grate of the Mongolian BBQ differs from the one in your back yard. It is basically a heavy slab of cast iron with narrow, slit openings about a quarter inch apart. I have a Mongolian BBQ grill, but it weighs so much that it takes two people to carry it. Such grills are not easy to come by and are probably fairly expensive, but don't despair: you can make a great Mongolian BBQ by using a large frying pan on your charcoal grill. Keep the frying pan oiled, and forget the fact that we Northern Chinese insist on using pine for the fire to give the food a special flavor. Charcoal will be just fine. You'll end up with a very tasty and novel dish that is very simple to make. I find it a great way to take care of a large number of people at informal dinners. Unlike a Mongolian fire pot, where the food is first boiled and then dipped into the sauce, the Mongolian BBQ requires that the raw ingredients are first mixed with the sauce and then grilled.

Use thinly sliced lamb and beef and roughly shredded vegetables such as carrots, cabbage, onion, green peppers, scallion, and bean sprouts. Mix the meat and the vegetables together in a bowl, about 1 part meat to 2 parts vegetable (as we do in stir frying).

Then add the following to taste: soy sauce, sesame oil, chilli oil, wine, ginger water (made by soaking grated ginger root in water), regular cooking oil and sugar. You'll want only enough sauce to marinate your food mixture, so try a ½ tbsp or so of each (less in the case of the chilli oil, or eliminate it altogether if you don't want the food to be spicy hot).

Dump the ingredients onto the grill or, more likely, into the frying pan and cook them as you would in stir frying. When done, scoop the mixture back into the bowl and eat it with a bread roll, stuffed into pitta bread, or rolled in a Chinese pancake. Your guests cook their own food while you sit back relaxing with a beer or a glass of wine.

Mongolian fire pot

This is a do-it-yourself dish, originating from Mongolia and common in Northern China. It is traditionally eaten in the winter and one of its attractions is that the cooking process produces heat (if you've ever been to Northern China in the winter, you'll appreciate the advantage of huddling around a source of heat).

The fire pot is eaten indoors and is essentially a water-based rather than an oil-based fondu. Charcoal is the source of heat. Smouldering in a chimney in the centre of the pot, it produces the heat to boil the water in which the food is cooked. A traditional charcoal-burning fire pot is not always practical. You can easily and successfully substitute a deep electric frying pan or any other electric pot which can hold around 3 inches of boiling water. The most traditional ingredients are thin slices of lamb, but you can use beef and assorted vegetables such as Chinese cabbage, any mustard greens that are available, bean curd or frozen bean curd and transparent bean noodles.

The sauce is a very important aspect of the fire pot. Since the food is cooked by boiling, the taste is bland. It is the dipping of the boiled food in the sauce that makes it so tasty. The sauce is a do-it-yourself combination of the following ingredients: soy sauce, sesame oil, chilli oil, chopped scallion or chives, shrimp paste, sesame paste, preserved red bean curd, Chinese parsley, sugar and wine. These ingredients are usually put in separate containers or bowls, placed together on a tray.

Mix together in a bowl a sauce combination that is to your taste.

Cook the raw meat and vegetables in the boiling water in the pot. They cook quickly, so don't let it go on too long. When your food is cooked to the degree you like it, fish it out, dip it into your bowl of sauce and eat away. Experience will improve your cooking and sauce mixing. You might want to begin with the following sauce combination: 1 tsp each of soy sauce, sesame oil, wine and sugar, plus chopped scallions. If you like it hot, add chilli oil.

As you cook, add water as necessary to replace the amount that is boiled away. Wait until the water boils again before you resume cooking. After a while, you'll have a good broth. It will be bland, though, and may need some seasoning.

This is a fun way to dine with friends and it's an easy way to enjoy some good eating.

The cup that cheers

Until President Nixon went to China, most Americans had never heard of Mao Tai. But when the United States official party and journalists who were with them on the visit had to drink toast after toast of Mao Tai at official banquets in Peking and Shanghai, the national drink of China quickly gained a fearsome reputation. "White lightning!" complained one bleary-eyed visitor after a banquet in the Great Hall of the People in Peking. It is a complaint that has been echoed many times since then with the huge influx of foreign tourists in China. Chinese love to drink when they are eating, especially in restaurants or during family feasts, and this is done with a sense of fun and competition aimed at getting the other people at the table tipsy. So, there are all sorts of games like the fingers game of rocks-scissors-paper after which the loser has to drain his glass, or another in which the head of a chicken or duck from one of the dishes is put on the middle of the circular serving area of the table. The turntable is spun around and whoever ends up with the chicken head facing him or her has to drink.

Then the host must toast his guests and the guests must toast the host and the youngest toast the oldest and so on. This is all done with much laughter and gusto and joy to the cries of 'kan pei' which roughly translated means 'bottoms up'.

So, kan pei!

Desserts

Desserts are a very weak area of Chinese cuisine. Baking or putting something inside an oven is simply alien to Chinese cooking. Traditionally everything was cooked on top of the fire. At home, the usual dessert is fruit. But there are two Chinese desserts that I would like to introduce to you.

EIGHT PRECIOUS TREASURES RICE PUDDING — STEAMED

This pudding gets its name from the rather exotic ingredients used. In Northern China, glutinous rice and candied fruits are a treat. In keeping with the Chinese propensity for flowery names, these are transformed into 'precious treasures'. The major ingredients are glutinous rice, canned sweet red bean paste — which you can buy easily in a Chinese grocery — sugar and shortening. To decorate this dessert, use candied nuts, dates, raisins, candied orange peel and, if you want, other more exotic ingredients such as candied lotus seed.

Wash 1½ cups of glutinous rice and add the same amount of water. Follow the recipe for cooking rice.

Place the cooked rice into a bowl and mix with 1 tbsp of shortening and 2 tbsp of sugar.

Generously grease a 6-inch diameter mold or bowl with shortening. On the bottom of the mold, artistically arrange the candied ingredients into a design.

Carefully spread 2/3rds of the cooked rice over the candied ingredients. Add ½ cup or more of sweet bean paste onto the middle of this and cover with the rest of the rice. Gently flatten the mixture and steam it for 2 hours.

Turn the mixture out into a deep platter.

Boil a mixture of ¾ cup of water, 2 to 3 tbsp of sugar and 3 tsp of cornstarch. Pour this over the dessert and serve hot.

ALMOND CURD OR ALMOND JELLY

Traditionally this dish is made with agar agar, but since this is a difficult ingredient to buy, we will take a short cut by using unflavored gelatin as a substitute.

Dissolve 2 packets of unflavored gelatin in 4½ to 5 cups of milk or 2½ cups each of water and condensed milk (this is more liquid than the gelatin instructions call for, but it will provide the softer texture that is characteristic of this dish). Add 3 tbsp of sugar (or to taste) and 2 tsp of almond extract. Mix well and pour the gelatin mixture into a flat glass baking dish, then refrigerate for at least 2 hours until the mixture congeals into a firm jelly.

To serve, cut the jelly into medium-sized cubes, put the cubes into small bowls, top with chilled fresh fruit cocktail, chilled canned fruit cocktail or chilled canned mandarin oranges.

Eight Precious Treasures Rice Pudding

Designed by PPA Design Limited

Printed by
Yu Luen Offset Printing Factory Ltd
36 Tai Yau Street, 1st Fl., Flat E & G,
San Po Kong, Kowloon, Hong Kong.